ADC

What's a Parent To Do?

Richard D. Parsons

PAULIST PRESS

NEW YORK/MAHWAH

Library of Congress Cataloging-in-Publication Data

Parsons, Richard D.
Adolescence: what's a parent to do?/by Richard D. Parsons.
p. cm.
ISBN 0-8091-2969-8 (pbk.)
1. Adolescence. 2. Parenting—Religious aspects—Christianity.
I. Title.
HQ796.P33 1988
649′.125—dc19 87-37587
CIP

Published by Paulist Press
997 Macarthur Boulevard
Mahwah, NJ 07430

Printed and bound in the United States of America

Contents

Acknowledgments

While many theorists and researchers provide the foundation for my work, the real "substance" and "life" of the book has been extracted from the lives, loves and struggles of the many parents and teens whom I have been privileged to know over the course of the last fifteen years.

The illustrations which are presented throughout the book reflect a composite of the various families with whom I have worked. All of the names and significant identifying information about the actual cases have been modified in order to insure the confidentiality of those involved.

In addition to those with whom I have had professional contact, support for this work comes from another source—Those special youths in my life: my sons, Kristian, Drew and Jonathan, and our special younger friends, Denis, Coleen, John, Michaele, Michael, Stephen and Lori.

There have been other people who have contributed to my growth as a parent, especially my friends and family, but a special thank you goes to Denis and Mary Ellen Spellman. As special friends they shared our joy of births, baptisms, birthdays and graduations and held our hands through operations, broken bones, and an evening of lost and found. It is in love that we shared our journey as parents with them, and with joy that we look forward to continuing that journey.

Dedication

For Karen, my partner, my friend, my love

She was with me at the beginning and I pray she will be with me till the end. We are family thanks to her gifts of love, joy and selflessness. So to my wife, Karen, I express my love and appreciation and dedicate this book to her.

Prologue

Even though it is well over fifteen years ago, I can still remember the day that I called my wife to let her know that the laboratory report had verified our suspicions. We were about to be parents!

Perhaps you also can remember the time and place of that special verification. That time when it was clear to you that you were about to become a parent. If you do remember that moment, then perhaps you, like me, can remember experiencing a wide range of thoughts and emotions which accompanied that realization.

Initially I was filled with excitement and joy over the thought of becoming a parent. Joy, however was not the only feeling I had. I became concerned and anxious over issues such as how I was to pay doctors' fees and hospital expenses and if I could, if I would, be able to be a good Christian parent. This apparent "tugging" of polar emotions, those drawing me toward the excitement and joy of the moment, and those pushing me away in anxiety, would be a preview of things to come.

Parenting certainly brings with it a mixing of positive and negative experiences and feelings. I am sure that like me you have experienced the speed with which the joyful cry of the newborn is replaced by the demanding whine of the 3 A.M. feeding. Similarly, many parents have experienced the joy and excitement of seeing a son or daughter preparing on prom night. How quickly these emotions become replaced by our anxieties about their abilities to make decisions of right and wrong during the long evening ahead.

Parenthood is clearly a wondrous and blessed life state. *Parenting* however, while most certainly wondrous, is often less than joyful. For most parents the stress and strain of parenting, while evident throughout the early years of child rearing, is magnified when they and their child enter the years of development known as "adolescence."

Adolescence is a time of much stress both for our children and for us. As parents of adolescents we need to take time to reflect on our own values, dreams, and experiences. We need to reflect on our growth as parents, as well as our shortcomings. We need to revive the intensity of love and enthusiasm for parenting that may have characterized those first few moments of seeing our newborn. And, finally, we need to increase our understanding of our youth and our skills of parenting so that we can assist our youth in this trying time of their development. It is in hopes of stimulating this reflection, renewal and increased understanding that this book is being presented.

There will be a number of issues discussed and themes presented in the chapters to come. As parents of adolescents we need to understand the adolescent experience with all of its stress and turmoil (Chapter 1). Further, we need to be able to provide the love (Chapter 2), the availability (Chapter 3) and the discipline (Chapter 4) that our youth require. In addition to a basic understanding of the adolescent experience, we need to be aware of the special issues confronting our youth today. As such the book will discuss issues such as family conflict (Chapter 5), sexuality (Chapter 6), drugs (Chapter 7), and peer influence (Chapter 8). There is, however, one theme that will underline each of the following chapters: that *Christian parenting is a ministry of special gifts and special demands.*

The task of Christian parenting is a valuable and responsible ministry. Like all parents who are given the responsibility and stewardship over children, Christian parents are required by the nature of their role to protect and nurture the development of the young. We are directed by our society to serve as the primary socializing agent. We are responsible to teach our children the "right" and proper ways of our culture. Hopefully this preparation will enable them to take up their place in this democratic society as fully functioning adults. To these ends most of us spend endless hours correcting our children's eating, playing, and speaking habits. Also we spend countless hours and hundreds of miles transporting our children to their instructions in dance, sports, and formal academics. But, as Christian parents, we are called to be more than providers, or agents of society. We are given stewardship over the early experiences and opportunities for our children's growth in order that we may foster their development in love of self, neighbor and God. The importance of this task is highlighted during the adolescent years.

Just as Christ emerged from childhood and began the work for which he was specifically called, so too, for our adolescents, this is a time to begin to hear the call and to respond in their own unique way. It is an appointed time, a time when each youth begins to etch out his or her own unique identity and lay claim to his or her values and beliefs.

As parents it is helpful to remember that God has "made everything appropriate to its time" (Eccl 3:11) and that the time of adolescence is a time of challenging and questioning, a time of testing and a time of emerging. Our calling and responsibility is to facilitate this process of growth and development so that each youth may be better able to know Christ and respond to his call.

To carry out our ministry we need to understand the experience of adolescence and become aware of those factors which contribute to the successful passage through this developmental period. Further, we need to develop the skills and attitudes necessary to become the "trusting stewards" and teachers of our children. Knowing how to set boundaries and protect, while at the same time letting go and allowing our youth the opportunity for self-governance and direction, is the task to which we as Christian parents are called to respond.

1.

Adolescence—A Time of Change

Moody! That only scratches the surface. He is completely unpredictable. Some days he's pleasant and cooperative. Other days he's like an angry bear, or isolated like a hermit. I give up—I just don't know what to expect anymore!

Adolescence is certainly a time of conflicting moods and motives, habits and dreams. Adolescence is a time of crises. It is a time when the old of "childhood" is being reassessed and replaced by the "new" of the emerging adult. And, as with any such period of reassessment and replacement, quite often that of the old, which is still "good" and "useful," is thrown out along with that which is no longer useful.

Adolescence is that period of development during which one comes to challenge and test all personal and social limits. It is a time to question tradition and experiment with new ideas and styles. As a period of questioning and challenging, it is a time of great stress and frustration for the adolescent and for us, their parents.

The sudden, rapid shifts in the adolescents' mood, manner and general style, their apparent rejection of family and family tradition and their struggles with making the right value-based decisions serve as major points of consternation for parents. It is a time when we as parents may wonder: "Where has our darling child gone?"

The Search, the Pain, of Identifying Me

The almost costume-like outfits, exaggerated hair style and manner, and loud-boisterous tone so characteristic of the adolescent are all signs of the adolescent's need for recognition. At times our teen appears poised and posed on center stage as if performing to the world. Other times the same youth will go to extremes to withdraw and retreat from the world. Either way, adolescents are most often absorbed in themselves, even to the exclusion of others, and others' needs. Each family expresses it in its own way: "Who ate the last donut?" "Are you ever going to get out of the bathroom?" "I am waiting for a phone call too, you know!" "Could you tune down the radio? We are trying to talk." Regardless of the form of the message it remains the same: the adolescent is involved, totally involved, in search of self.

The main business of adolescents is finding who they are and who they are to become, a process called ego identification. During this period the youth tries to build a self-concept which appears accurate and functional, a self-concept with which he or she can live. The question of identity and the concern over the issue of "who I am and where I am going" doesn't start at adolescence, nor will it necessarily end when the adolescent emerges into adulthood. We all need to stop and ask the question: "Who am I, and where am I going?"

I recently had my forty-first birthday, and while I can protest all I want that I am "above" (or is it beyond?) any life crises, it was clearly a time of reflection. This anniversary of my birth was a time of introspection and reevaluation of who and what I had become over the last forty-one years. Like the adolescent we often take time to reflect and reevaluate the "who" we are. Unlike the adolescent, however, our reevaluation and reidentification appears to occur with much less fanfare and trauma. Why then is it so traumatizing and so much more difficult for the adolescent?

Ask a child to answer the question "Who are you?" and you might get a response such as the one I received from my own eight year old: "I'm Jonathan. I'm eight years old and in second grade. I like to play soccer, computer games and ride my bike. My friend is Jon. I live in Thornbury and I'd like to be an artist." Similarly, and with as much ease as shown by the eight year old, I found that I answered the question noting that "I am a psychologist, married with three children, and I work at a local college. I like to play tennis and lately I am getting into working with my hands. I enjoy writing, need to lose weight and I am looking forward to a sabbatical!"

Most likely your response to the above question will prove quite similar to mine. Just like the eight year old, most adults identify "who they are" by pointing to specific references such as job, marital status, sex role, etc. Adults and children respond to the question of identity with the same type of response. "Self" for these two groups is often defined and tied to referents such as one's biological or physical traits (overweight, male), social roles and status (second grader, and psychologist) and personal evaluations and reflections on qualities and aspirations (likes, dislikes, dreams). Since these reference points are relatively stable our response to the question of "Who am I?" remains consistent over time.

Why then is it so difficult and obviously so painful for the adolescent to respond to the same question of "Who am I?" For the adolescent the self is blurred and the previous referents which served the child as points of sameness and continuity are no longer dependable. Rather, the youth finds that these anchors, these stable referent points, are changing rapidly without his or her control and without any clear vision of when and where the changes will stop. No longer a child and not yet an adult, the adolescent without the sense of stability to body and body image, or social role and status, is oftentimes overwhelmed by anxiety around the issue of "Who am I and where am I going?"

This anxiety is clearly reflected in the self-description voiced by one youth.

> It is like I am living in a bad dream, a nightmare. I look in the mirror and I am not sure whom I am looking at. My body changes all the time; my face looks different; it sometimes feels as if it is somebody else's body. I hate it! I have no control. You know you can laugh over things like pimples, but they are painful; they are ugly. I'm ugly.
>
> The experience is not just the physical thing. I mean even my friends, my family, are changing. Things that used to be fun no longer seem to work for me. Everybody treats me differently. They seem to be changing all of the rules. Sometimes I am told to act like an adult. "Grow up!" they say. But then

> when I make decisions that are adult-like, they jump down my throat. I am supposed to question things when it comes to my friends. "Don't just follow the crowd," they say. But God forbid if I question them. All I have to do is ask my parents why I have to go to church, and they hit the roof. Could you imagine what would happen if I told them I was questioning whether there really is a God. They would die!
>
> It really is scary. I don't look the way I used to. I don't act the way I used to. Things I used to enjoy are either no longer fun, or I am too old to do them! Perhaps the most scary of all is that things I never questioned (such as whether there is a God) are issues which are no longer so clear. It scares me because I don't know how it will all turn out, what I will become. I really wish I could just wake up and everything would be the way it was!

The confusion, turmoil and felt crises of this youth are shared by all adolescents in varying degrees as they go through the process of reidentifying and redefining "who they are." As parents it is not only helpful, but perhaps essential that we begin to understand the actual and somewhat predictable changes which the adolescent is experiencing. By understanding these changes and the developmental tasks confronting our children we will be better able to provide the support and care they need during this period of storm and stress.

The Tasks of Adolescence

As we move through our life journey we are confronted with a variety of tasks. These tasks are set by one's cultural milieu, or by oneself as a biological organism, or by the interaction of the cultural and biological factors we experience. Many of these tasks take on crucial dimensions in that they need to be accomplished or achieved if one is to develop normally. The adolescent is confronted with developmental tasks, each aimed at providing a fuller, more clear sense of self. While various theorists may identify a more or less developed listing of tasks, most agree that adolescents in their attempts at developing their own unique identity, their own special sense of self, must:

1. Come to terms with their own body, accepting their physique and learning to use their body effectively.

2. Learn the appropriate sex roles, what it is to be a male or female in our society/culture.

3. Develop mature, effective relationships with their peers of both sexes.

4. Achieve emotional independence from their parents and other adults and begin to move toward social-economic independence.

5. Prepare for a vocational/occupational future.

6. Develop a system of values, and ideals which will guide their actions and decisions.

The "business" of adolescence is serious and the youth's attempts to resolve each of the previously mentioned tasks needs to be understood. Such attempts to resolve any one of the above tasks may take a variety of forms. For example, the adolescent attempting to come to terms with his or her physique may give extra attention to nutrition and hygiene, or may turn to the more self-destructive reactions such as anorexia or bulimia.

The process of addressing these tasks is often one of trial and error. This process brings with it many potential dangers, real and perceived threats, and a wealth of opportunities for growth. Thus it appears important that we understand these tasks and the various ways that young people attempt to resolve them. As parents of a teen, you and I can find some comfort from our anxieties by understanding the challenges presented by each of these tasks. Such an understanding will help us to appreciate the difficulty experienced by our adolescents and the "normalcy" of their actions. This understanding will also help us to assist our teenagers to cope with each of the demands.

While each of the tasks is discussed in the upcoming chapters, two of them are particularly pivotal for adolescents in their process of resolving the question of identity. The two tasks discussed below reflect their need to come to grips with their body and bodily changes, and their need to establish appropriate social peer relationships.

New Body—New Me?

The transformation of a child into an adult is announced by the less than spectacular signals of puberty. Cracking voices, erupting skin, fuzzy chins and budding breasts are all announcements to the world that our adolescent children are moving into the biological world of the sexually mature. The physical changes which accompany this biological event are only a small part of the experience of puberty.

Along with the physical changes comes the redefinition of the adolescent's self-identity. As suggested earlier in this chapter one of the primary "anchors" for defining one's identity is the body image. "I'm a boy," "I'm tall," "I'm not so strong," are all components of the ultimate identification of who "I" am. And the body image with which the child had become so clearly identified and so comfortable now undergoes radical and sometimes frightening changes during adolescence.

> "Look at these pimples—they're disgusting. I'm disgusting. Who would want to go to the dance with someone like me?"

> "It isn't fair. Everybody in my class is starting to shave. What's wrong? Am I weird? Am I gay?"

> "I'm not going to gym—no way. Those guys will make fun of me."

As parents of an adolescent we are often frustrated by our inability to gain access to the bathroom which has been under siege by our sixteen year old. Similarly, many parents have been frustrated by their inability to ease the pain experienced by their youth who has equated a "pimple" with the "end of the world." Quite often our attempts at assuring our daughter that she is as pretty as ever, regardless of the "zit" on her nose, or that our son is sure to be as big and as strong as his friends, and that he is just a little slower in his development, prove quite ineffective. Further, our attempts at relieving our teenager's distress with a word of encouragement are often met by an outburst of tears and anger and the claim: "You just don't understand—nobody does!"

It is hard for me, and most likely for you, to truly appreciate the felt lack of control and absolute crisis experienced by the adolescent whose body is going through such rapid change. Unlike the adolescent we experience our bodies as relatively stable and slow to change. While I may be frustrated by the fact that I know in order to lose weight I must exercise and watch my diet, and that such a process will take some time, I am comforted by the fact that I feel I can control the process and predict its outcome. For the adolescent, however, it is not so simple. The adolescent feels as if his or her body is on a journey of its own, without his or her control and without any hint of its final destination. Things seem to change on their own, oftentimes overnight. Our sons and daughters may know where they would like to go, be it to lose weight, gain muscles, have more (or less) body hair, bigger or smaller breasts, etc., but they are without any reasonable plan to direct such changes. They feel as if they are left to the "whim" of their own body.

This sense of lack of control is one ingredient contributing to the frustration that the adolescent experiences. A second ingredient is the teen's tendency to equate the body, with its various states of undesirability, with the "self." Thus for a youth it is not just the body, but also the "self," which is viewed as out of control, often directionless, and unacceptable. As such, adolescents will devote endless hours attending to their appearance in an attempt to gain control over the ultimate direction and outcome of these changes of body and "self."

This absorption can often be quite frustrating to the apparently helpless parent. I remember the call from one frantic parent who announced that she was about to "kill" her daughter. It appeared that after two months of prom dress hunting, an expensive visit to the hairdresser, and the frantic search for shoes and accessories, when prom night came her daughter announced that she was not going. "How do you expect me to go looking like this! My hair is a mess, my dress is the wrong color and look at these pimples! God, they are all over my face. It's disgusting!"

The parents' attempt to rebut their daughter's claims proved totally useless. The "But, Hon, your hair is perfect—the dress makes your eyes look bluer, and nobody will notice that one pimple on your forehead" only elicited more tears and the embittered cry of youth, "You don't understand!"

Not being in her shoes at that moment, I can concur that I don't understand. Looking at her child at a time such as this, she sees a lovely person. Granted there is a pimple, but from her vantage point it seems that makeup or an adjustment of her hair could hide that blemish. The problems simply don't seem to be so catastrophic, nor so difficult to resolve. The difficulty is that, as parents, we are attempting to deal with problems which are only *conditions* of our daughter's appearance—the color of her dress, the arrangement of her hair, and the existence of a blemish. She, however, is attempting to resolve a condition of existence, who she is. It is not as simple as having an ugly pimple; it is that *I am* the pimple, and it is I that am ugly, unacceptable. From this perspective all of our attempts to gloss over this imperfection miss the mark. Stating that it "is no big deal" simply fails to reflect the intensity with which she feels threatened.

I have found that it is often more productive to accept our child's perception of a problem as catastrophic with the hopes of moving him or her to a problem solving orientation. "Wow, I guess that does bother you. That pimple is gross. Is it painful?" Often such a reflection of the youth's perspective moves him or her to clarify exactly what things are problematic and to what degree. Rather than spending time and energy arguing the philosophical nature of beauty, it would be better to align ourselves with our child in order to creatively reduce the negative effects of this "ghastly looking thing."

In accepting our adolescent's perspective, a parent might respond: "I know you must be disappointed. It is really a shame to miss the prom after all your friends are going and your hair and gown look so attractive. I wonder how we could hide that pimple." Such an approach quite often elicits a problem-solving attitude from our youth that will be more effective in resolving the immediate crisis. This is not to suggest that we are trying to play mind-games with our teen. The point is that from a position of sensitivity and empathy we may more fully appreciate the intensity of the crisis felt by the adolescent when assaulted by such biological events. Even though the real resolution rests in assisting our adolescent to separate the value of self from the conditions of self (e.g., how one looks), this lesson is better learned after the crisis has passed.

It is not just the period of crisis which requires sensitivity on the part of the parent. Adolescents, while they may smile and attempt a good-natured response to ribbing about their cracking voices, their fuzzy chins, or their womanly figure, still experience anxiety and discomfort over these changes and are in need of sensitivity.

In addition to having an empathic understanding regarding our youth's experience of biological changes, it is important for us to have accurate information regarding the bodily changes to be experienced. We need to provide our youth with this same accurate information. We can help reduce much of the anxiety surrounding these changes by helping our teen to understand the effects of hormones on body and emotions, the normal variations in growth and the temporary nature of these conditions.

Myself, My Friends, My World

> "They tell me to act my age, and when I try to, when I try to make decisions for myself, they freak out on me!"

> "Sure, on the one hand I'm supposed to make up my own mind, you know, don't simply follow the crowd but make my own decisions. But if I challenge or question them, watch out!"

> "Eighteen is old enough to die for my country, but I can't even get a beer if I want to, or even decide at what time I want to come in at night. Talk about mixed messages!"

The voices of the youth presented above reflect the real sense of frustration and conflict which each adolescent experiences as he or she moves from childhood to adulthood. The biological accompaniments of puberty clearly announce to youth that they are moving from childhood, but their destination is not always as clear or as cleanly defined. At various times our youth will find themselves placed in the demands of adulthood, yet without the accompanying rights and freedoms. As individuals of "marginal" status, living in transition between the world of the child and the world of the adult, adolescents turn toward one another to find the stability and consistency of a social world not provided by those adults around them.

To the consternation of most parents, our adolescents' peers become the most important people in their lives. No longer is the family picnic, or visiting grandmother, or going to a game with dad, the most important event in their lives. A Sunday dinner at home could never compete with a concert and friends, and a family night at the movies is no match for a couple of hours at the dance, at the mall, or at so and so's house. The old connections and investment with family are being replaced by connections with peers, and so it should be.

The intense attraction to peers is twofold. First, "misery loves company." The adolescent finds comfort in sharing the same uncomfortable and marginal position as one's peers. Second, our youth do constitute the generation of tomorrow. They need to relate, to be with one another, to etch out their special roles, since they are the society of tomorrow! As with the other areas of development, the adolescent starts out by overemphasizing the value of peers to the exclusion of reasonable thought or proper social behavior, but this too shall pass. The unending hours on the phone, the conflicts surrounding each new adventure in love, the experimentation with dating and drugs, are all part of the process of identifying and solidifying mature social relationships. As such, it is important that our youth begin to establish meaningful relationships with same and opposite sex peers and begin to identify the value and need for social rules and roles.

Adolescents, while desiring to belong, will test the limits of society. They will question and challenge all our rules and regulations. They will also question and challenge the rules and roles of their own peer society. In testing the social limits, our youth will begin to understand the value and need for social rules and roles. In addition, this testing of limits will bring with it times when they are forced to stand alone with their values against pressure from their peer society. This pressure can be very powerful and our youth will need our support to stand strong. The potential power of your youth's peers is an issue which deserves special attention and is discussed more fully in Chapter 8.

Why Now, Lord?

As with any such time in life, adolescence can be viewed as an "appointed" time. Adolescence is a time of identity achievement. It is a time when adolescents attempt to identify *who they are* and *who they are to become,* especially in light of Jesus' invitation to "come, follow me" (Mk 10:21).

Their journey is certainly one with many highs and many lows. The tasks confronting adolescents as they travel through this phase of their life bring with them much anxiety and concern for teens and parents alike. It is a marvelous, mysterious journey through which adolescents need much support and guidance.

As stewards over those experiences which impact our youth we are called to respond to this "appointed time" in a way which will ease their journey in search of self and God. While there will be many frustrating moments in the journey—moments when you may ask God "Why now?"—it is important to remember that God has "made everything appropriate to its time" (Eccl 3:11) so that what might at first appear to be a disaster is really an invitation to growth.

Parent Points

- Adolescence is a time of stress and turmoil.

- The primary source of conflict for our teens is the uncertainty and instability of their self-concept. Who they are and who they are to become are the central questions of the adolescent experience.

- The adolescents' "self-concept" is under attack! Two primary components of their self-concept, their body image and their social position, are in upheaval.

- Teens' overconcern with their physical appearance and their being accepted by peers is their attempt to gain some security during this time of crisis.

- With all of the changes and uncertainty facing our youth, they need the stability of caring, understanding parents.

- Our teens need to experience adults who are sensitive and empathic to their fears and anxieties.

- Our teens need accurate information regarding the physical changes they are experiencing.

- Teens and parents need to remember that our Lord is speaking to us, even in the midst of struggle and crisis. Adolescence is a time of struggle. It is also a time of invitation. We are all invited to grow through this struggle. We are invited to reassess who we are, and who we are to become, especially in light of Christ's invitation to "come, follow me."

2.

Unconditional Love: The Primary Ingredient of Christian Parenting

You must love one another just as I have loved you. It is by your love for one another, that everyone will recognize you as my disciples.

(Jn 13:34)

My years as a parent and as a clinician counseling parents and their children have helped me to appreciate that parenting is not only a very difficult and highly responsible role, but also one in which our priorities, values and perspectives are often easily subverted and confused. While working with families in crisis, where there are intense negative feelings and often overt aggression exhibited between parents and their children, I often find myself asking "Where has the initial excitement—joy—wonderment that these parents surely felt upon the birth of their child—gone?" "What has happened to the awe and respect the child once held for his parents?" How do we destroy these positive feelings and replace them with mutual hostility and disrespect?

All too often we allow ourselves to become distracted from the love and joy we felt when introduced to the miracle of life by the day to day pressures and stresses we face. We are often barraged by concerns and issues needing our immediate attention. These issues may distract us from the real responsibility of parenting—to love our children. Our concern about establishing a workable budget, planning for our future or simply coping with the daily demands of monitoring homework and mediating sibling squabbles may assume priority.

Our role as Christian parents is one requiring much more than simply acting as providers or agents of our society. We are called to foster our youth's development in love—love of self, love of neighbor and love of God.

Models of Love

Children learn to love both themselves and others not by instruction and verbal command but by the modeling they receive. Christ provides us with the model for teaching this love. While Christ most assuredly taught and preached love, he also lived as he instructed. As parents we need to consider if and how we live the messages we preach:

- Do we live out the messages, and the life style that we demand of our youth?
- Do we *respect* them, as we demand their respect?
- Do we afford them our undivided attention as a sign of prizing and valuing them, as we require their attention to our spoken words of wisdom?
- Do we provide them with the consistent, unconditional love, they truly deserve or do we hold out our love as a prize to be won only when they perform for us?

Providing *unconditional love* through *acceptance* and *non-possessive warmth* is essential for the development of the healthy, spiritually mature individual. Without the experience of unconditional love and the resulting acceptance of one's own worthwhileness, it is hard, if not impossible, for one to develop a mature sense of love of neighbor or God.

Acceptance. As new parents, we experienced many long nights of frustration and inconvenience. During the early years it was almost expected to have our sleep disturbed by a crying child. Similarly, most of us experienced the interruption of meals as a result of spilled milk and other such accidents. Even with such adversity we maintained our love, our absolute acceptance of our child, just as he or she was. As our youth enters adolescence we may find that the accidents, disruptions, and interferences of this age (the late night telephone marathons, the disheveled rooms, the unusual dress and makeup) often elicit quite a different response. Quite often we may find that our responses may signal our *non-acceptance* of our youth rather than a dissatisfaction with the particular event or condition. In trying to understand and maintain such total unconditional acceptance we should remember that the acceptability of our youth ultimately comes from God. By the virtue of their creation they *are* acceptable. Their acceptance by God should certainly assure our less consequential acceptance. This is *not* to imply absolute, wholesale approval of everything they do and say. To the contrary, simply expressing an "it's O.K. attitude" about everything they attempt is simply a way of expressing radical non-involvement or non-concern. If you really care for them, then you will extend yourself in the hope of educating, motivating, and easing their growth. The accepting parent is able to distinguish between the absolute unconditional acceptance of the adolescent and the non-acceptance or even rejection of their behavior.

In addition to feeling this acceptance, we must learn to convey it to our youth. Most parents, like myself, assume that their children know they accept and love them. My experience as a clinician points to the opposite, however. Many children fail to see the subtle signs of love exhibited by their parents. Often a teen selectively remembers and highlights only those experiences of displeasure exhibited by his or her parents. Further, many youth take their parents' negative responses as evidence that they are angry, upset and rejecting them as people rather than simply upset, angry and rejecting what they have done. The comment "I can't stand it when you do that" is all too often heard as "I can't stand *you*." The laughter or sarcastic comment made about a teen's manner of dress is all too frequently received as a put-down of the person, and not simply of the clothes.

To combat this faulty perception we must demonstrate our acceptance of our youth as persons by attending to them as they share their ideas and perspectives and showing them care, respect and concern as they share their problems. It does little to *say* "I love you" if we are willing to listen and discuss their concerns only *after* the game is over or "I've finished the paper."

Non-Possessive Warmth. In addition to acceptance, unconditional love is manifested in our ability to prize and value our youth in a non-possessive way. Our adolescents need to know that we appreciate them and value them because they are human beings, and not simply because they are ours (as if they were possessions or trophies) or because they have achieved some accomplishment.

All too often we vacillate in our feelings for our teens based on their performance, moving from feelings of negativity and neutrality to those of warmth and pride. It is as if we value them only when they get good grades or win a competition. How stark is the contrast to those early days of parenting when we would proudly smile and flash pictures of our infants simply because they "were," not because of what they "did." If our valuing is based on performance, then it is *not* valuing of the person. Rather, it is valuing of the achievement. When our youth perceive such a conditional valuing, they will fear the loss of value in our eyes, should they ever fall short of the mark or fail in the competition.

When we exhibit non-possessive warmth we reflect to our youth our deep, non-evaluative respect for their thoughts, feelings, wishes and potential as free and responsible individuals. This prizing is a true reflection of our Christian belief that each individual is created in the image and likeness of God, endowed with natural gifts in varying degrees of development. It is the foundation of the message to love our neighbors as our selves.

As with true acceptance, unconditional prizing or valuing of the person does not imply unconditional liking or approval of all that our children do. Just as Christ was able to love the sinner while hating the sin, we should learn to distinguish our evaluation of our children's behavior or actions from the love and value we hold for them as our flesh and blood.

While each of us, especially during the early days of parenthood, experienced such unconditional acceptance and prizing of our infant, many of us may find it difficult to continue to express such unconditional love for our oftentimes rebellious youth. We may find that we are conveying conditional love through our use of words spoken in anger, such as "I hate you," "You make me sick," or "I am so ashamed of you." Even those phrases we assume to be positive such as "I am proud of you for doing . . ." can convey conditional prizing. It is important, therefore, to consider those conditions which inhibit our expression of such unconditional acceptance so that even in the face of extreme disappointment, we may remain, like the father of the prodigal son, strong and steady in our love, and willing and accepting of our youth.

Faulty Beliefs—A Destructive Force

When I think about my early days of parenting I often shudder and then laugh at the lack of understanding and foolish expectations I held regarding children and their development, and my own role as parent. One particular experience during those early years of parenting still remains quite clear and poignant to me. During the first few months following the birth of our son, Kristian, my wife took quite ill. As a "liberated" male, I attempted to extend myself to help with our child wherever I could. During one particularly stressful night, when I was trying to soothe the baby and quiet the cries, I found myself calling out in frustration to my wife, "You're a woman; you know what to do!" My wife, being extremely understanding and charitable (not to say also too ill to come and wring my neck), responded by stating, "You know, Rick, this is my first baby too!" The power of her statement that night has done more for my own mental health and approach to life than she will ever know. It was with her words that I began to recognize the source of most of my frustration, anger and sense of impotence experienced as a parent. These negative feelings were not a result of unending cries of distress coming from my child. These feelings stemmed from my own ridiculous, non-functional, and unreasonable belief regarding the way the world (or in this case, my child) *should* or *must be.* As I became aware that the world was not the way I demanded it to be (that is, quiet and sleeping) I immediately concluded that it was *unfair* that such a thing would be happening to me, and that it was so *unbearable* that I *could not stand it!*

I am sure most of you have experienced events which you viewed as totally unfair and intolerable, and that in your "wisdom" you, like me, have made rules for the way the world should be. For example, "The person in front of me in that car *has no right* to go so slow! Wow, that makes me mad."

The point of the above is to demonstrate that it is not the world that makes me mad, it is not the baby crying, or the person driving slowly, but rather it is *me* that makes me mad. By incorrectly interpreting these events as being more important and more threatening than they really are, I have taken incidents of minor inconvenience and turned them into extremely unjust catastrophes. And so it is with our parenting and our interaction with our children.

The Many "Shoulds" of Parents. Whether it is by accident or design, we have come to hold a number of attitudes and beliefs which, when used to guide our behavior, most often prove counterproductive.

For example, many of us firmly believe that our children *must* respect us, *must* tell the truth, *must* do homework, etc. By now you are probably thinking, "Yes, so what? There *are* certain things which our children, which we, *must do!*"

If we could meet face to face, I would suggest that there is really nothing that any person must do. We *do not have* to pay taxes, or mow the grass, or go to work, or anything for that matter! As adults, however, we recognize that choosing not to do certain things will result in a number of consequences. Further, as adults, we conclude that if we wish to avoid certain things such as going to jail, having our house overrun with weeds and perhaps sleeping in the street, then it makes sense to do each of the above. The point is that while we use the word *should,* we really believe and mean "It is preferable," "It is desirable" or "It is, given the options, what I *want* to do."

While it may appear that I am simply playing with words, I cannot emphasize enough that it is not the words which concern me but the very firm, almost rigid beliefs which they may reflect. Further, it is the negative effects of such rigid and dysfunctional beliefs that concern me the most.

Perhaps an example would help to highlight the importance and potentially destructive nature of such thinking. Consider that you just placed your three year old daughter in bed. You settle into your favorite chair and begin to read the paper. Suddenly you hear a loud, terrifying scream come from your child's room. Rushing into the bedroom you see your child sitting up in bed, trembling as if completely and utterly terrified. When you ask what it was that frightened her, she most likely responds that it was the dark.

Most parents, myself included, would accept this response and try to allay her fears by stating everything is O.K. and that she is safe. On closer inspection, however, your child's response really makes little sense. If she was afraid of the dark, then it would seem that she should exhibit this terrified reaction every night. Yet such has not been the case. It is not the darkness which created the fright, but the child's belief that the noise she heard in the dark was evidence that a *monster* or some *horrible thing* was going to get her. The child's inaccurate though strongly held belief serves as the source of her terror, not the darkness. The sadness of this scene rests in the fact that not only does the child experience an intense negative emotion, fright, but does so as a result of her own misinterpreting and distorting of reality. While her reaction might be totally appropriate if there truly was a monster, it is inappropriate given the reality of a simple floor board popping.

The monsters of childhood are not lost in childhood, however. The irrational and unreasonable way we all interpret reality not only places us in extremely uncomfortable emotional positions, but quite often contributes to our poorly thought out and oftentimes destructive reactions. Therefore, truly believing that my son has no right to question my statements or directives leads me to interpret his challenge as arrogant and bold. With this perspective I may respond punitively, in anger. However, if I see his questioning and challenging not as a refusal to adhere to the eleventh commandment, "Thou shalt not question thy father," but rather as his attempt to develop independence and self-governance, then I may be less angry and more oriented to resolving the issue at hand, rather than escalating the challenge to a point of personal conflict. Learning to challenge my *musts* and *shoulds* and reinterpret these as wants, wishes, or desires provides me with the energy needed to direct my efforts to attaining what I want.

Perhaps another example may help to clarify this point. I can remember being outside, working on a Saturday morning, trying to straighten up a neglected yard. I saw my adolescent son in the house relaxing and I convinced myself that he didn't have any right being in there and that he should be out helping me. Further, firmly believing that he was not fulfilling his obligation, not doing what he should, I then concluded that he was a rotten kid who needed to be punished. Such an internal dialogue would most likely result in my becoming angry so that when I addressed my son I would have done so with much hostility and disrespect. It would have been much more desirable if I could have challenged my thinking by asking myself, "Why should he be out here? The fact is, I am here because I want to be. I would rather be working in the yard than have the yard a mess. Why then is he rotten for doing what he wants?"

By such debating, I could have realized that I didn't have to be angry, hate or punish my child; he is not a rotten person. Further, I would have seen that rather than believing that "he should be out here helping" the real issue was: "I want him to help me!" With this reorientation, I would have also come to realize that if it is I who want something (my son to help), then it is up to me to get him out here. From such a problem-solving frame of reference I might begin to consider the various ways in which I could *motivate* him to help. I may consider a variety of solutions, ranging from simply asking, to offering some payoff, etc.

While the issue of discipline is discussed in more detail in Chapter 5, the point here is that holding on to irrational beliefs such as these *shoulds* and *musts* will prove detrimental to my own happiness and will most likely lead to responses which are detrimental to the development of a healthy, caring and unconditionally loving relationship with my child.

Parents Must Be Perfect. In addition to the many *shoulds,* and *musts* we lay on our children, many of us hold similar *shoulds* and *musts* regarding our role as parents. One special *should* which creates havoc for a parent is: "I should be the perfectly competent parent!"

Parents who firmly believe that they must be or should be totally competent and adequate are parents who are the prime breeding ground for debilitating guilt and anxiety. If I believe that I must be perfect in order to be adequate and acceptable, then I am setting up an impossible expectation (no one is perfect). Further, such a belief sets the stage wherein each decision becomes anxiety-provoking. If my decision is wrong, it is not a matter of simply making a mistake. Rather, it is my "value" as a parent, as a person, which may be on the line.

Such parents are like the Monday morning quarterbacks who in retrospect not only see what they did wrong, (e.g., "I should never have grounded him," or "I know I should have been more strict") but unjustly punish themselves for not having the foresight to have made the right, the perfect, decision all the time. Such self-beating is unreasonable since we did the best we could, given our knowledge, perspective, demands, etc. Further such a process is self-defeating in that the energy we use to punish ourselves with guilt or create anxieties about the next major mistake we will make drains the energy we need to cope day to day with the problems being presented. Parents who firmly hold on to the belief that it is all their fault and that they should have been better parents need to challenge their thinking. It is almost like saying, "If I knew then what I know now, I would do it differently." Of course we would. The reality, however, was we didn't know then and as such we did the best we could, given what we had to work with.

The Need To Be Rational

As Christian parents, as rational parents, we need to fight these *shoulds* and *musts.* We need to replace them with statements of *wish* and *want*. For while it is motivating to try to be the best you can be, it is unrealistic and unhealthy to demand that the best be perfect and that anything less is unacceptable.

Learning to accept ourselves, with our limitations and failures, provides us with the basis from which to accept our teens, even when they are less than perfect. We need to accept that we are imperfect and live in an imperfect world. Even with such limitations, we have value and worth which were bought for us at the highest of all prices, the death of God's Son. With this as our belief, we will be able to become better parents and assist our children in their own striving for growth. We will be able to do this without ever wavering in our underlying unconditional acceptance and valuing of ourselves and our children.

There is much to teach our adolescents, but the greatest lesson of all is to love! All other lessons will be for nought if we are unable to show our children healthy consistent love and thereby facilitate within them a sense of unconditional worthwhileness.

Parent Points

- At this juncture of our parenting we need to take time out to reflect on the joy that was ours at the birth of our teen. Do we still feel that joy?

- As parents of teens we must attend to many important tasks such as assisting with homework or overseeing curfews and manners. All of these tasks demand our time and energy. We must not, however, allow these tasks to distract us from the most important thing of all—*love!*

- Often we are distracted from our experience of love and joy by the many big and small tasks, conditions of parenting. We need to question whether this or that task or chore is so important that we should allow it to create negative feelings between ourselves and our teen.

- It is important to remind ourselves and our teens that our love for them is *not* based on what they do for us. It is *unconditional.*

- Often we assume that our teens know that we love them. Such is not always the case. Be sure to express that love!

- Using Christ as our model of love, we need to live our love, not just verbalize it.

- Unconditionally accepting our children means that we:
  **respect them;

****give them our attention when they need it;**
****see beyond their hair, clothes, friends, and grades and accept the person inside.**

- **Unconditionally accepting our teens *does not* mean wholesale or blanket approval of all that they do. For just as Christ could hate the sin while loving the sinner, we need to discriminate between our dislike of actions versus our liking for the person. We need to learn to say and demonstrate: "I love you, but I don't like the way you are acting!"**

- **Our teen is a gift—a gift to be prized, a gift of joy. We need to remind ourselves of this value and demonstrate our joy.**

3.

Hearing—Listening—Understanding

Honest, I try. I say, "Talk to me," and she just walks away. I think that I am available, that I am open—but we just can't *communicate.*

It is often stated that the primary problem between the generations is their inability and/or unwillingness to communicate with one another. As a parent of an adolescent I have found times when I felt that my son was speaking a foreign language. There have been other times as I tried to explain something to him that I thought perhaps it was I who was speaking in a strange tongue.

Most of us have either experienced or could imagine experiencing the same type of frustration reflected in the above quote. However, we might be quite surprised to find that the quote, while certainly applicable to our own parenting experience, was actually expressed to me by an adolescent. Frustration regarding a felt inability to be heard is not unique to parents. Our youth often experience the same type of frustration and conflict in satisfying their desire to communicate, to express their needs, to their parents. The communication gap is experienced as equally painful on either side of the line. Just as parents are quick to note that our children "no longer share with us," our youth retort that it is we who "no longer listen" or have the time for them. The adolescents with whom I speak note the difficulty they have in expressing their feelings, their concerns, their aspirations with their parents. They note that it is not just difficult for them to identify their feelings and concerns but almost impossible to share these difficult feelings with their parents. This communication is particularly thwarted when we as adults interrupt, proselytize and patronize them.

The Communication Gap—A Sign of the Times

Problems with intergenerational communication are not unique to the 1980's. Adolescents, teens, the younger generation have always found new and somewhat cryptic means of communicating among themselves, as if to exclude the older generation from participating in their world. The use of terms and phrases such as "gay," "dude," "cool" and "bad," along with the heavy reliance on non-verbal communication through use of hand gestures, emblems, clothing, etc., was as evident in the 1930's, 1940's and 1950's as it is today. I have found it both enlightening and quite enjoyable to watch adolescents express surprise when their parents share some of the special words that characterized their generation. Our youth are even more shocked to find that *the* word and/or gesture which they thought their parents were too weird or square to understand has been used for many generations.

Many of us have suffered hours of torment and anguish as we become increasingly aware that our once "literate" and "articulate" child has become the grunting, mumbling adolescent. Over the course of an hour, we may listen in amazement to a telephone conversation in which a minimum of words are exchanged. Such a transition in communication style and focus is both a natural and desirable accompaniment to the adolescent's drive toward independent, adult status. As our teens attempt to increase their independence, they actively begin to exclude the other generation from their life, from their society. In their attempt to increase the integrity of their own society, our teens develop ways and means of increasing their privacy. This is done by spending more time with friends and less with family members, and also by withholding information or speaking in their own somewhat secret language.

The gap brings with it a number of minor conflicts regarding hair style, musical tastes, length and frequency of phone conversations, missing dinners, and the ever-present failure of our youth to tell us what's going on. These conflicts, however, need not continue nor need they be the cause for discontinued contact and understanding within the family.

A Time To Speak, A Time To Listen

In order to understand the language of the adolescent we must begin to understand the needs experienced by our youth. We need to translate their actions and their expressions in light of these needs. From such a perspective we will come to realize that often it is not so important that we *speak* and provide our youth with our insights, or our words of wisdom, but rather that we attend and listen to our youth. Even though our adolescents need to receive instruction and direction, most youth report that what they really want is to be heard, to be listened to, to be understood.

Thus the essential ingredient of communicating with an adolescent lies in our ability to do much more than simply *hear* them. It is essential that we begin to learn to *listen* to our teens in such a way as to truly come to *understand* their adolescent experience. With this understanding we will be better positioned to bridge the communication gap. Listening for understanding requires that we listen with our ears, our eyes, our hearts, our very beings. This form of active, involved listening is a skill which does not come easily, but it is one which is essential to the accurate understanding of our youth.

To Listen Is To Attend

I can think of many occasions during which my mother and dad were attempting to communicate some information regarding my chore for the afternoon. Quite often they would ask me almost in mid-sentence whether I was listening to them. Like most youths I would be quick to respond that of course I was listening! Further, I can remember the number of times when I could hear my father or mother talking to me, and I would be able to provide the appropriate number of "yeahs," "huh, huhs" or "O.K.'s" even though I was fully engrossed in my television viewing.

As humans we have the unique ability to hear and temporarily store information with very little energy and/or attention. Perhaps you could remember a time when you were able to smile and appear socially responsive to someone giving a long and less than stimulating speech. We smile as if attending, while all the while we are mentally planning the rest of our day. All too often, however, this type of hearing and superficial responding is equated with listening and communicating. And, sadly, such "communicating" is often the hallmark of the listening which characterizes parent-adolescent exchanges.

Effective listening requires our full physical and psychological attention to the other. It is an active, oftentimes exhaustive process which demands time and energy.

Physically Attending. Research on communication has time and time again reinforced the value of body posture and positioning as a means of sending signals to another, as well as a means of facilitating or inhibiting the accurate reception of another's message. Consider, for example, trying to talk with your son about a topic of deep concern. As you begin talking you notice that your adolescent begins to look away, slightly turning his head and upper torso away from your direction, and slowly nestling down in his seat as if to take a brief snooze. Unless you have the patience of Job, you will most likely stop trying to discuss the point at hand, feeling perhaps a bit hurt or angry at your teen's inattention.

The feelings of frustration, annoyance, or hurt which you have experienced are in response to the body signals your child is sending. Clearly, the lack of eye contact, and the failure to be open and straight in line with you as you speak, suggest that your child is not interested in what you have to say.

As I write this I can remember the times I frustrated myself by asking my son to take out the trash or do some other such chore. I would stand beside him (rather than in front) with a clear view of his head (not his face and eyes) while he physically attended to the TV. I would then become surprised by his lack of responsiveness to the request and shocked to hear him say that he didn't hear me!

If we want to listen to and understand our youth, we must begin to learn to position ourselves in a manner which encourages our own attentiveness to the other's message. A posture characterized as a straight, open body position, in which there is a slight forward lean in the direction of the speaker and the maintenance of eye contact, has been found to increase one's attentiveness. The relative simplicity and perhaps obvious quality of such a S.O.L.E.R. (straight, open, lean, eye, relaxed) posture may lead us to give it lip service (e.g., "Oh yeah, I knew that") without really employing it in our day-to-day interactions. To emphasize the potency of this posture I would suggest that you attempt the following mini-experiment. On an occasion when you and a friend, spouse, or teen are talking on some topic of concern, consciously and deliberately take up the S.O.L.E.R. body position. That is, sit, straight in line with the speaker, keeping your arms and legs comfortably apart, leaning slightly in the other's direction while maintaining a relaxed degree of eye contact. As your partner begins to speak, start to deviate from this facilitative posture. For example, perhaps you could slowly begin to look away (thus breaking eye contact) or slowly rotate your body, head and shoulders away from him. It won't be long until your friend stops his line of discussion and asks if something is wrong. More significantly however, as you move from the facilitative posture you will find it more difficult to attend to the real message your speaker is conveying. You will find that you miss some of the subtle cues that help you to understand what he is really trying to convey to you (e.g., facial expressions, gestures, or shifts in body position). You may even find it more difficult to avoid attending to other distractions such as the TV or a person passing nearby, to the exclusion of any reception of your speaker's message.

Without belaboring this point, it is important to remember that simply taking up such an attending position when we wish to listen and communicate with our youth will facilitate our accurate reception of their messages. Further, our body position will really convey to our youth our desire to *be with* them in this conversation. Like all other such techniques the value of the S.O.L.E.R. positioning can be undermined if it is forced and contrived. While I am encouraging each of us to use such attending as much as possible I am not suggesting that we need to rearrange the room, reposition the chairs, or go through any extraordinary efforts to establish such a S.O.L.E.R. position when communicating with our youth. Rather, we should keep the model in mind as we begin to communicate with our adolescent and attempt, as naturally, and as comfortably as possible, to achieve it.

Attending Psychologically. Even after we have become skilled in the use of the SOLER position, we may find ourselves having difficulty fully attending to our teen. Quite often such difficulty is a direct result of our trying to be quiet, polite, passive listeners.

As youths most of us were instructed to be quiet, polite listeners. While such directives can be instructive in terms of reminding us not to be interruptive or judgmental, they are misleading if we conclude that listening is therefore a passive process. Attempting to be passive listeners often leads us to become momentarily distracted.

Like me, you may have experienced an occasion in school or at a meeting or lecture when during a long-winded presentation you found yourself temporarily absorbed in your own personal fantasy or concern. Obviously such self-absorption and distraction will interfere with an accurate reception and understanding of the speaker's message. And so it is in communicating with our youth. If we attempt to remain totally silent and allow our youth to ramble, we will not be aiding in communication. In fact we will be making true, accurate communication more difficult.

In order to reduce this non-attendance we must learn to become active, empathic listeners. As an active listener you will have to involve yourself in the gathering of information. You will need to periodically interrupt your youth to summarize what it is you hear being said. This summarization will enable you to check your reception for its accuracy. Further, you will need to step out from behind your own perspective in order to see the world from your teens' point of view. Seeing the world as they do will facilitate your accurate reception and understanding of their message. For example, your sixteen year old announces that even though he spent over one hundred dollars for the ticket, flowers and formal attire, he has decided not to go to the prom. He further announces that his decision was the result of his girlfriend announcing that she only wanted "to be friends" and not "go steady." Our temptation as parents might be to weigh the expense of the evening against the less than traumatic news and thus direct our youth to "go or else!" While it is clear that the parents who respond in such a manner have heard their youth, they failed to understand the entire message. It is not only the *money* and the *friendship* at stake, but it is also the *pride*, the *grieving of a love* and the potential *humiliation* which he is trying to convey and for which he seeks some help. For us to completely and accurately understand the message, we must learn to listen to more than just the words. We must begin to listen to the underlying tone. We must begin to try to place ourselves in their shoes, to understand the real impact of what is being conveyed. When listening to our youth, it is important that we keep their perspective in mind. We can keep their perspective in mind by asking, "What is the message they want me to receive?" "What would it be like if I were in their shoes?" "What would these words mean to me and what would I be looking for by way of a response from my parents?"

Another technique which can help us psychologically attend and stay in tune with our teens as they speak is to try to accurately reflect the content and feeling we hear. Such a process requires that we periodically interrupt our youth and *reflect* to them the message which we are receiving. For example, your teen announces "The dance is coming up and I really don't know who to ask (laughing nervously). You know, there are so many possible choices (looking down, dropping his shoulders)." If you use reflective listening and preface any advice giving by summarizing and reflecting the message or messages you have received you might note: "It seems to me that you are not only having some difficulty about choosing a date for the dance. I also sense you are not too sure about how successful you are going to be." Such a response will not only convey your attentiveness to your youth's message, but your reflection may assist the teen to identify the real issue at hand, which in this case may be the youth's felt inability to attract a date.

The intent of this response and the use of a reflection is not to play mind reader or psychologist, but to simply and accurately reflect to your youth that you are *really* attending. Further, your response lets your teen know that you want to know if the message you are perceiving, is the one the youth intended to send. As such the parent provides the adolescent with a reflection of the *essence* of what was said, along with the implied message conveyed by the *manner* in which it was said.

Such active listening is a very powerful communication tool. Because of the adolescent's own inability to explicate feelings and concerns, the parents with the ability to read between the lines, go beyond the words and extract the meaning underneath the overt message not only will better understand their youth, but will be better able to respond.

As humans we are naturally communicative, but good and accurate communication is not always natural. It is important to practice actively listening to our youth. It is important to find the time and the energy to physically and psychologically attend to their messages. Further it is important to provide our teen with evidence of our desire (even when limited in ability) to be present and available. It is through such presence and availability that the communication gap can and will be bridged.

Parent Points

- As humans we are naturally communicative, but good and accurate communication is not always natural!
- As communicative animals we are always communicating. As parents we need to be alert and open to the subtle messages conveyed by our teen.
- To bridge the generation gap we need to improve our reception, our listening skills.
- We must learn to listen with our eyes . . .
with our hearts . . .
with our very beings.
- We need to break out of the passive role of listeners and become actively involved in reaching out and understanding what our teens are trying to convey.
- Being with our teen is essential. Such attending can be assisted if we employ proper attending behaviors.
- S.O.L.E.R.—being straight, open, with a slight lean toward the speaker, keeping eye contact, all in a relaxed style, sets the stage for accurately receiving the information sent to us by our teens.
- In addition to physically attending, we must remain psychologically attentive and involved. Using active listening, periodically interrupting our youth to summarize what we have received and check it for its accuracy, will help us to truly understand what is being conveyed.

- **Being empathic and learning to listen beyond the words to the emotional message (past the tune to the tone) will add further understanding.**

- **Learning to consider what is being said from our teens' perspective, asking ourselves, "What would I be meaning if I were in their shoes?" is essential to the development of this empathy.**

- **Being present, available, and understanding are the essential components to communicating with teens. Instructions and guidance are elements which will flow once the generation gap has been bridged.**

4.

Discipline—Firm and Kind

Parents, don't keep on scolding and nagging your children, making them angry and resentful. Rather, bring them up with the loving discipline the Lord himself approves.

(Ephesians 6:4)

During the question and answer period of a workshop I recently presented, a man sitting in the back of the auditorium raised his hand and asked: "Tell me, is discipline *in* or *out* this year?"

Is discipline *in?* My response to that parent was: "Discipline has never been *out!*" However, the reaction which followed cautioned me that much more needed to be said about this issue of disciplining. "Oh, great," he responded. "You mean we can now go home and beat our kids without feeling guilty?"

All too often discipline and punishment are equated. Even though punishment might be considered a disciplining act, it is not the complete definition of discipline nor necessarily even the most effective form. *Discipline is any kind of experience or training that leads to a correction, modification, shaping or strengthening of a certain behavior.*

From such a broad definition of discipline it is clear that discipline could *never* be out! Consider, for example, the process your daughter goes through as she learns to become proficient on her skate board. Each time she falls off the board, she makes an adjustment to her positioning and balance. Falling off the board and successfully riding it are disciplining experiences. Similarly, whenever you begin to modify your golf swing or back hand as a result of hitting a poor shot, you are demonstrating the effects of being disciplined by the experience of poor performance. Finally, the adolescent who begins to change his eating habits, study regimen, or room-cleaning behavior as a result of some experience—regardless of whether it is the internal sense of pleasure that comes with losing weight, obtaining better grades, or having a clean room, or from the external pleasure of having his parents, teachers, or peers praise him—has been disciplined.

Therefore the question that we need to have answered is *not* whether it is O.K. or not O.K. to discipline but rather how we as Christian parents can effectively discipline our children so that what is corrected, modified, strengthened or trained is aligned with our own Christian values and our desired goals for parenting.

Rules Are Needed—
And Need to Be Changed

As newborns, our children were quite vulnerable and in need of almost constant care and protection. As parents we provided our infants with clear safe limits. We took our responsibilities seriously and attempted to provide our children with the external guidance and control which would insure their happy and healthy development.

With time our children started to give evidence of our nurturance. They would begin to stand alone, take those first few steps and announce to the world that they were ready to test their boundaries and limits.

As parents we viewed each of these milestones of independence and self-direction as evidence of our own parenting success. Why, then, do we view our adolescents' signs of independence and maturation as threats to our authority rather than evidence of our successful parenting? Why do we so often respond to our youths' testing of their boundaries not with applause and support but with tightened grips of control?

The first time our child challenged our dictates by saying "no" to our request to share her toy or clean up his room may have come as quite a shock. The clash of needs (our need to have them share or pick up the room with their need to continue playing) often resulted in our increased demonstration of force. "Do it or else!" may have been our response with "Because I said so!" as our justification. Quite often the raised voice and stern look proved quite effective in resolving this conflict and providing us with what we wanted (e.g., a clean room). However, the same approach, when applied to our adolescent son or daughter, not only seems less efficient and effective but most likely will prove quite detrimental. Parents who rule with an unchallenged iron hand, laying down rules and regulations without explanation or discussion, are sure to experience some form of adolescent rebellion. In situations where the rebellion is not evident, the youth may be following the rules simply out of fear. Such an unhealthy acquiescence will result in stunted growth toward self-direction.

This is *not to imply* that extreme permissiveness or lack of limit setting is desirable. Rules need to exist. Knowing the real limits to acceptable behavior and understanding the consequence of violation of these limits is essential for our teens' social and moral development.

Rules are needed, but rules need to be tested, challenged and changed. Just as our child changes, grows and develops, the specific need for rules and the types of rules and guides which will prove helpful need to change, grow and develop along with their ability to be self-governing. What is being emphasized is that we need to recognize the importance of self-direction. Further, we need to provide our teens with the maximum degree of freedom which they can *safely* and *successfully* employ. Our adolescents need to know and experience that as their parents we are responsible for them and as such will continue to be involved in the process of limit setting. At the same time, however, our teens need to understand that we believe that they are gaining in their own self-control and as such we expect and encourage them to contribute maturely to the development of these personal limits.

Skills and Attitudes

St. Paul (Ephesians 6:4) reminded us that it is not good to employ negatives such as nagging or scolding to rear our youth, but that rather we should employ *loving discipline.* Loving discipline is a discipline which is both *firm* and *kind.* It is a discipline which requires both the development of specific parenting skills and the possession of an appropriate, loving attitude.

While there are a number of excellent parent-training programs and skill development texts written on the topics of behavior modification and discipline, all too often this material fails to discuss the important role which parental attitudes and style play in effective Christian parenting. It has been my personal and professional experience that while we often understand the concept of effective discipline, we fail in our implementation because of our own ineffective parenting style or the dysfunctional attitudes we have regarding our children and child-rearing.

As noted in Chapter 2, parents, either through accident or design, often possess a number of attitudes and beliefs which when used to guide their interaction with their children most often prove counter-productive. As noted in that earlier chapter, when we *firmly* and somewhat *stubbornly* convince ourselves that our children *have no right* to challenge or question our parental rules, we set ourselves up to perceive their natural and healthy testing of the rules as a sign of their arrogance and total disrespect. From such a perspective we often respond to their "testing of the limits" with anything but loving discipline. Providing the firm yet kind and loving guidelines needed by our teens requires identifying and challenging our irrational attitudes and beliefs about parenting. We need to question those various *shoulds* and *musts* (for example: children must take out the trash, must be nice to their siblings, must love and respect their parents) which we have uncritically accepted as guiding principles. As we question these beliefs, we may come to realize that while all of the above tasks are *desirable* acts they fall short of being absolute or life-determining.

The point of this discussion is to help us all recognize that the actions which we believe are essential musts are more accurately actions which are functional, desirable and preferable. Further, it is important for us to realize that what is desirable is really a function of what the individual sees as desirable.

Consider the case of the never-ending battle of the trash. While it may be true that the trash in my kitchen is piled three bags high, this is not evidence that my son must take it out or that he is lazy for not doing his duty. This monument of trash has most likely become quite an irritant for me, and it is because it is so annoying to me that I am motivated to have it removed. My son, however, is clearly unaffected by the presence of "only" three bags of trash. Thus since it doesn't bother him, and since he is more annoyed by the inconvenience of taking it out, he will be less motivated than I to have it removed. There is nothing natural or sacred to motivate a fifteen year old to take out the kitchen trash. In fact, on closer inspection I soon come to realize that my son, just like me, is motivated to do things which he wants.

This knowledge and perspective helps me to change my attitude both about my son, and about what needs to be done in this particular situation. No longer will I see my son as a lazy, no-good bum who needs to be punished for not doing what every kid is supposed to. Rather, I will begin to see that my son is just like me. He responds to such tasks as taking out the trash only when the consequence warrants such action. That is, I was motivated because the sight of the trash annoyed or irritated me and thus its removal would have proved pleasing. Similarly, my son will be motivated to remove the trash, when either the sight of it becomes annoying and/or the removal becomes pleasing. From this perspective I find that I am motivated to find a way to have my son do what I *want,* rather than sitting passively and perhaps angrily waiting for him to do what *he should.* Further, from such a perspective I find that I no longer become infuriated with his resistance as he responds, "I'll get it in a minute." I remind myself that it is I who want it removed, not he. He is not being disrespectful but simply avoiding doing something that he is not particularly interested in or excited about.

Skills and Guidelines for Disciplining

In order to implement the loving discipline St. Paul speaks of, we not only need healthy and appropriate attitudes, but also the skills, as teachers, to effectively shape, modify and correct our children's behavior. To be effective in our disciplining we need to be clear, calm and consistent while using cues and consequences to guide our teens' actions.

Be clear. One of the first rules or guiding principles of effective disciplining is to be clear and concise in describing what it is we want our adolescent to do or not to do. Often we establish rules which are vague and open to misinterpretation and then find ourselves getting angry when our teen fails to comply. For example, telling my adolescent to be home at a *reasonable* hour is sure to invite a number of interesting definitions of reasonable. This is not to suggest that we need to get overly legalistic, because that can be a trap as well. I am just suggesting that we attempt to be clear and concise in our description of our rules and regulations. Further, we need to check with our children to insure that they accurately understand the rules and the consequences for failing to abide by the rules. I can remember an incident which I had with my middle son, Drew, that made this point very clear to me. It was during the Christmas season and I, like hundreds of other last minute shoppers, was attempting to finish my Christmas list in a very crowded and hot mall. Drew, who was five at the time, navigated along with me through the various crowds. We were quite pleased with our shopping success. I mentioned to Drew, as we entered one last store, that he had been very good and helpful and that if he would *behave* in this last store, we would treat ourselves to some snacks. As I was considering the final gift, a flash of awareness washed over me. Drew was no longer by my side, but I could see him racing up and down the store as if he were in a *grand prix.* Gathering my composure, I paid for my last gift, reclaimed my wandering son and exited the mall. As we left the store, Drew looked up, apparently quite pleased with himself, and asked if we were going to get our treats. What followed was a barrage of parental clichés, starting with: "A treat, after how you behaved! *All I asked was that you behave, and you . . .*" After I had ventilated all my frustration (about shopping) on this innocent by-stander, he quite poignantly said, "But Dad, I did behave!" His loving smile and simple words were presented in all sincerity and innocence. The truth of the matter was that he did behave. From the perspective of a hot and tired five year old, "behaving" meant not bothering dad, not breaking anything and not yelling or hurting anyone. From his definition it was clear that Drew did behave. How was he to know that I meant that he should stand by my side, not breathe, not look around or even think about touching anything. His innocence and insight not only helped me to relax and gain perspective that day, but also allowed both of us to enjoy the treat we deserved.

Give Cues. Since the ultimate goal of our disciplining is to teach our children how to make mature, responsible decisions about their actions, we need to discipline in a way that will help them internalize our direction and methods of control. For example, when your adolescent was a toddler, he or she may have found the electric receptacles as an object of interest. If they approached the wall, reaching out to the socket, you most likely said: "No, no, don't touch—bad" or some other verbal cue. Further, you may have accompanied this verbal cue with the parental wagging finger and the shaking head, all implying *don't touch.* Finally, if your child continued on his or her quest, and reached out, you may have intercepted the child's hand and smacked it firmly, saying "No, No!" The sequence described points to the importance of the cues we provide in teaching our children how to anticipate a consequence of their actions. If we continued to observe our child we might find that he or she returns to the outlet but this time at the approach we may notice the head shaking "no, no" and the hand being pulled back as if you were by his or her side. Typically our verbal and non-verbal cues, once paired with either positive or negative consequences, take on new meaning and provide our children with a mechanism of internal control.

So it is true for parenting our adolescent sons and daughters. They, like the toddler, are curious. They want to know what happens if they stay out beyond the curfew, experiment with this or that, or simply refuse to do what they are asked. If our goal is to teach them self-control and responsible decision making, then we need to warn our adolescents, providing them a cue as to the consequence of their decision prior to their decision. Failing, for example, to let them know that they are crossing the boundary from being assertive to being disrespectful or from showing responsible driving or dating habits to being irresponsible and then simply punishing them for their eventual rule violation is not helping them to make responsible, consequential decisions. We need to help them recognize that they are about to violate a rule, and further asisst them to redirect themselves in order to gain control. This becomes especially important when a family discussion or conflict starts to exceed the boundaries of rational discussion and problem solving. When during a discussion teenagers begin to approach disrespect or unacceptable behavior, rather than simply allowing the discussion to continue to disintegrate and then punishing them for acting so unacceptably, we need to provide them with a warning, a cue that their behavior is becoming unacceptable. A statement such as "That's enough," "Let's stop," "Time-out," or some other phrase that signifies that they need to consider their action and make an appropriate decision in order to experience the desired outcome is an essential component in teaching our youth to become responsible, consequential decision makers.

Demonstrate the Consequences. Most of us are familiar with "Grandmom's principle," that is, if you eat your peas, you can have your dessert. Grandmom not only knew how to motivate us to eat our peas (at least on those days we wanted dessert) but she also taught us the importance of consequences as a motivating force. When our children were small we most likely provided them with hugs, kisses, smiles, words of praise and even little treats as rewards for doing something which we wanted. By the time they reach adolescence, however, we begin to act as if they no longer want, need, or deserve such rewards for doing what we want them to do.

All too often we operate with the principle "Never wake a sleeping baby." That is, when our teens are doing what we want them to do, whether it is to do their homework, take out the trash, or clean their room, we often fail to praise them, fearing that we will rock the boat or that it really is unneeded since they are simply doing what they should. However, we are quick to punish them for not performing such duties.

One of the simplest rules in psychology suggests that if we follow a behavior by a pleasing outcome, then that behavior will tend to be repeated. Therefore, in order to discipline our adolescent in such a way that he or she begins to perform certain desirable behaviors it would make sense to follow the performance of these behaviors with some positive consequence. While a reward may be thought of as something like a treat, money, extra free time, or added privileges, it may be as simple and as natural as a parental smile and word of thanks.

For many of us, however, the thought of providing our teen with an extra payoff for doing a chore simply rubs us the wrong way. If you find this to be true for yourself you may want to consider the possibility that your feelings regarding providing such rewards stems from your belief that it is your child's duty to do these acts and therefore he or she *should* simply do it without reward. While I wish this were true, my experience and most likely your own suggests that our children do not simply do these actions. And as previously noted, it really is not an issue of should's or duties, but more an issue of wants. It wasn't my duty, for example, to eat my peas, but I soon found that I wanted to not because of their own intrinsic worth or taste, but because of the consequence which would follow.

It is often around this issue of consequences that parents will ask about the use of punishment as a motivating consequence. As St. Paul noted, use of such techniques may result in our children becoming angry and resentful. Most modern research supports St. Paul's observation. It has been demonstrated that sole reliance on punishment as a disciplining consequence not only fails to change the behavior but may actually lead to the development of even more unacceptable behavior. For example, many parents employ "grounding" as a motivating consequence. If the grounding becomes excessive, then the threat of future grounding has little effect (I am already grounded for a year; who cares?). Furthermore, the adolescent may find that it is easier to escape by running away or sneaking out than it is to endure the punishment. Thus what is learned is how to break additional rules and avoid consequences and what results is more violation and perhaps the escalation of more punishment.

Because of the potential problems and dangers with such reliance on punishment, I suggest that if punishment is to be used, it be used rarely and only in mild form. Further, since the benefit of punishment is that it temporarily stops the unacceptable behavior from occurring, any hopes of changing the behavior requires that we accompany our punishment with an opportunity for our youth to perform the desired behavior, which in turn will be followed by a positive consequence. For example, if your daughter stayed out beyond curfew, after clearly understanding the rule and the potential consequence, you may decide to punish her by grounding her for the next weekend. It would prove much more effective in terms of disciplining to suggest to your daughter that while grounding is the punishment incurred, her performance of some other desirable behavior (for example, babysit without complaint, do extra helping around the house, or extra studying) could work off the punishment. By pairing such a desirable behavior with the removal of punishment, a parent not only increases the desire and strength of these positive behaviors but also provides the youth with an acceptable alternative to avoiding the punishment as opposed to running away or escaping.

Be Consistent. All of the previous discussion regarding cues and consequences will prove useless if the youth is unable to predict with any consistency how such cues are in fact precursors to certain positive or negative consequences. Thus it is essential that we attempt to be as consistent as possible with our rule and rule enforcement. This does not mean that we should be rigid, unchanging and perfectly consistent, but rather that our rules, cues and their consequences should not fluctuate with our unpredictable moods, or whims. Consistency in their environment allows our teens to make the needed predictions about their world and the possibilities confronting them. Teens who are unable to predict a parent's rules or reaction to rule violation may either become so anxious that they refuse to test any of the limits or, alternatively, learn to gamble that perhaps this will be a time when they can get away with an unacceptable behavior.

Be Calm and Caring. As noted in Chapter 2 the essential ingredient throughout our parenting efforts is to keep our perspective of unconditionally loving our youth. When we approach the establishment of rules and regulations and then attempt to implement them with cues and consequences, we should do so in a calm, caring manner. It is in approaching our youth in a calm, caring way that a message of love and concern is conveyed.

Yelling, screaming, and attacking will only teach our youth that we are angry and out of control. Further, the intensity of our emotions often acts as a primary distractor from the message we are really attempting to teach. Consider a situation in which you have "run a red light" and are now being pulled over by a police officer. The rule of the red light is quite clear, as was the cue. Similarly, you are most likely aware of the consequence, and while unhappy with the situation you are most likely rebuking yourself for rushing, rather than simply abiding by the law. However, as the policeman approaches the car you find that he is beet red and is screaming and hollering obscenities about you and your driving. It is clear that for some reason your violation of this driving law has infuriated him to the point that he is emotionally out of control. Under such a condition you will most likely forget that it is you who did the wrongdoing and be distracted by the potentially dangerous and anxiety provoking reaction of the policeman.

The same type of distraction is presented by the parent who, after waiting for ninety minutes beyond the expected time of their son's or daughter's arrival home, greets the youth at the door, screaming: "Where the hell were you? I was worried sick!" Under these conditions the youth will most likely fail to appreciate the real love and concern the parent feels. The reddened face, the loud, and forceful yell and the use of profanity acts as quite a distractor from this underlying message.

Be Firm but Kind. We generally don't view Christ as a disciplinarian, but who else has assisted so many to correct, modify, strengthen or change their behavior? As we attempt to integrate the various skills of disciplining along with the functional, Christian attitudes of parenting, we may find it helpful to turn to the model of Christ to guide us. Christ as a model of love was firm in his articulation of the "rules" but kind in his application. Christ set before his disciples not just instruction but a living example of his instruction. As Christ taught, so he lived. He preached, loved, and was our best living example of love.

The importance of style and modeling can not be overemphasized. Many of us rely on a style of parenting which emphasizes being *firm*. We are excellent at setting rules and regulations. Further, we often establish as our parenting priority the achievement of obedience and blind acceptance of our dictates. Such parents most often employ punitive, coercive, forceful methods of rule implementation. Parents who employ such a form of discipline may find their rules followed but the cost may be great. It is not unusual for adolescents raised under such an environment to not only develop a detachment from their parents, feeling hostile and negative toward them, but also may learn to treat others as they have been treated. These youth often become disrespectful and insensitive to the needs of others and likewise tend to rely on the use of threat, power and punishment as their primary form of interacting with others.

There are other parents who, in an attempt to avoid the creation of such negative feelings within their child, bend over backward to be *kind* and avoid frustrating their child. These parents avoid setting any consistent limits, and when limits are pronounced, their violation goes without enforcement. Such extreme permissiveness is just as damaging and stifling to mature, Christian development as is the overly autocratic, punitive approach. A child reared under such permissiveness is often without control and direction. These children begin to expect that others in the world will attend to all of their needs and meet all of their demands. These youth are not only setting themselves up for a rude awakening, but in the process exhibit an extremely self-centered, self-serving style and often alienate themselves from their friends and the rest of the world.

As caring, Christian parents, we need to temper our *firmness* in rule setting with the *kindness* and *concern* for the legitimate needs of our adolescent. It is important that we believe in the legitimacy of our teen's needs and desires, while at the same time affirming our own responsibility to guide.

In order to assist our adolescents in learning to both live and love the law, we will need to provide them with the opportunities to share in the law-making process. Conflict between what our youth may want, and what society or we determine to be appropriate, is going to be inevitable. Parents with the appropriate skills and Christian attitude, however, will be able to address these conflicts in ways which promote growth for themselves and their teens.

Parent Points

- Our teen, regardless of age, needs discipline. Rules are needed, but they need to change as our teen's ability for self-governance and self-direction increases.

- The need to discipline is *not* the same as the need to punish!
  **Punishment does not change behavior; it will only temporarily inhibit the expression of that behavior.
  **If punishment is used, it should be mild and always paired with an alternative acceptable means of removing the punishment.
  **Sole or extensive reliance on punishment (e.g., grounding) as a means of discipline may be destructive to the parent-child relationship. As St. Paul noted: "Parents, don't keep scolding and nagging your children, making them angry and resentful. Rather, bring them up with loving discipline the Lord himself approves." (Ephesians 6:4)

- Loving discipline requires parents to be both *firm* and *kind.*
  **Loving discipline requires the rational, loving, attitude of a teacher—the ability to remain *calm* and *caring.*
  **Loving discipline requires parents to be *clear* and *concrete,* employ *cues,* provide desirable *consequences* for desirable behaviors, and attempt to be *consistent* in the application and enforcement of the rules.

- As Christian parents we need to temper our *firmness* in rule setting with *kindness* and *concern* for the legitimate needs of our adolescent.

5.

Family Conflict— Who's Going To Win?

Point—Set—Match!

I never knew that when I became a parent, I would also have to become a "Solomon," wise in all my judgments. Overseeing the various sibling arguments over issues such as "who touched whom first," or "who had what first," or even "whose turn it is," requires not just the wisdom of Solomon, but quite often the striped shirt of an NFL referee or the loudspeaker of a Wimbledon judge! Listening to argument followed by counter-argument leaves me feeling that I should intervene with the announcement: " . . . and the winner is!"

Conflict within families is not restricted to squabbles between siblings, nor is it always so innocent as to be limited to arguments regarding who gets to see which TV show first. I have found that what often starts out as a small conflict between parent and teen may explode with much fury and destructiveness. An exchange that starts "Dad can I go to the mall?" moves from the response "No, not tonight; I need you to stay around the house" through a strange set of escalators, distorters, and polarizers, and ends up with comments such as "I hate you!" or actions such as physical attacks.

Conflict within families is inevitable, but it need not result in such destruction. Conflict can be a source, an opportunity, for growth and increased intimacy. The negativity and destruction which accompany family conflict is a result not of conflict itself, but of the manner in which it was handled.

The current chapter focuses upon a number of the more common pitfalls surrounding the resolution of conflict and provides one model for constructive conflict resolution.

Conflict between a parent and teen will exist whenever either the parent or the adolescent perceives that what is wanted is incompatible with what the other person wants. A mother who is on the phone talking to a friend will find herself in conflict with her daughter who wishes to use the phone. Conflict will also result whenever either the parent or the adolescent perceives that the other party is interfering with the achievement of a particular goal. One such goal interference might be when our teen is unable to meet that special friend because "dad won't let me use the car!" Yes conflict is inevitable but it is not inevitably destructive.

PITFALLS TO CONSTRUCTIVE CONFLICT RESOLUTION

Learning to creatively respond to conflict can result in a close, problem solving bond between parent and child. The process of identifying our needs and creatively working together in problem solving can provide a basis for increased communications between parent and youth and strengthen the relationship. Such creative responding requires that we maintain the proper perspective and employ appropriate conflict resolution skills. The first step in creatively responding to conflict is to identify and avoid the more typical "pitfalls" to constructive conflict resolution.

These pitfalls are many and are often unique to each family and even each incident of conflict. My own experience working with families in conflict has helped me identify three of the more common pitfalls. These three pitfalls, *Polarization* (Me, then you), *Escalation* (The Big Bang!), and *Use of coercion* (Might makes right) are discussed below.

Polarization: Me, Then You

Dad: "Ah what's the big deal anyway? You can always see her tomorrow. I want to relax."

Daughter: "Dad, you watch football every Sunday. I have to meet the gang at the mall. It's important!"

Exchanges like the above are commonplace and are found in many households on any particular Sunday in the fall. What appears to simply be a matter of two individuals expressing their wants may in fact be an opportunity for them to grow in the relationship. The statements along with their apparent incompatibility and potential for conflict provide both dad and daughter the opportunity to come to know more about one another and to work together in resolving the conflict.

The youth's request to go to the mall was an opportunity for dad to understand more about his daughter's friends, the role of peers in her life and even the part played by the mall in her adolescent society. Similarly, the youth might have found that a few strategically phrased questions might have taught her much about her dad's youth, his own involvement with sports and friends, and the special role that TV sports play in his life.

All too often, what could be an opportunity for sharing and growing in problem resolution results in polarization and becomes a cornerstone for increased hard feelings and emotional distance between parents and teens.

I find that parents, myself included, often fail to appreciate or value their children's needs, wishes or desires. We often view their requests as unimportant, unessential, and perhaps even frivolous. Somehow, our activities, be they watching the sporting event on TV, reading our book or finishing our cross stitch is important, whereas our daughter's desire to go to the mall, visit a friend, or practice her driving seems less important. A natural consequence of our tendency to view another's needs or wants as less important or essential than our own is the development of an attitude and position of *polarization (Me, then you).*

With such polarization comes the attitude that we are *absolutely* right and justified in our request, whereas our teen is clearly wrong, or perhaps simply silly. Compromise or attempts at mutual satisfaction will not be considered. Rather our goal will be to seek self-satisfaction and simply ignore or discount the request of our youth.

It should be obvious that we parents are not the only parties guilty of such polarization. Our youth with their built in "self-centered" view of life find it very hard to value and appreciate the legitimacy and felt importance of our adult needs. With both parent and teen isolated in our own world of needs, estranged or alienated from the other, we begin to operate as if each conflict is a "you versus me" situation.

Learning to work together in constructive conflict resolution requires that we begin to appreciate that the legitimacy of one's needs is not a result of the person's age, intelligence, income, or social status. The fact that I am the wage earner or the adult does not mean that my desire to feel comfortable, or read the book, or relax is any more legitimate than my adolescent's desire to do the same. We need to view our children's request from their perspective so that we can appreciate the intensity and felt importance of their need. If we can appreciate their need and their right to satisfy that need, then we will most likely be willing to seek resolutions to the conflict which will be mutually satisfying.

Escalation: The Big Bang!

Each of us has probably experienced the loss of perspective and the escalation of a minor point into a major confrontation. Thankfully, most of us have been able to regain perspective and renew the relationship with our teen with little damage done. I can remember an incident I had with my own son, Drew. Drew, a fourth grader at the time, came down from his room and proudly announced that he had finished his homework. He asked if I would like to see his answer to his social studies question. I was quite pleased at both his interest and excitement over the homework and his willingness to share it with me. I read the answer and praised him for both his style and content. So far so good, but the story doesn't end there. Like many parents, I sometimes fail to let things well enough alone. I began to look over the original question in his textbook. As I read the question I realized that it was seeking a multiple answer, stating: "Explain the reasons for . . ." I pointed out to Drew that while his response was super it was only one reason and that the question asked for reasons. I said, "Drew, I think you should develop another answer showing at least two reasons." Drew responded: "Dad, she (the teacher) only wants one answer." From this starting point, the exchanges seemed to come quickly and more intensely to a point where I was about to ground Drew for not following my directive. I found myself shouting, "Go do your homework correctly!" Happily, the light of rationality went on and I realized that I was about to make a tragic mistake. What started out as an opportunity to praise my son for his homework effort, and to show him that I was interested in his schooling, had become a real battle of the wills. And rather than escalating it to the point of explosion I was able to stop in mid-sentence and apologize for the way I was acting. I suggested to Drew that we wait and see how the teacher reacted to his homework in order to tell if his one excellent answer was sufficient. Thus what was almost a point of emotional destruction was averted.

Such is not always the case, however. All too often what starts out as a minor point of disagreement escalates to the point where physical blows result or irreversibly damaging words or threats are exchanged. Incidents such as parents expelling their teens from their homes or teens running away in anger often stem from what appears to have been a manageable point of conflict.

Dad: "Well, what time can we expect you?"
Son: "Well, ah, how about 12 o'clock?"
Dad: "Make it 11!"
Son: "Why? Everybody else is staying until 12!"
Dad: "You're not everybody else. I said 11!"
Son: "I can't believe you. You got to ruin everything. I never . . ."
Dad: (interrupting) "You'd better believe me. I'm your father, and if you don't knock it off, you can forget about going out all together."
Son: "Who cares! What's the use if I have to be in at 11!"
Dad: "Fine! Then you can just forget about it, and if you give me any more lip, you can forget about the rest of the weekend."

Son: (mumbling to himself) "Who cares. It never fails. I never get a break. I just ought to leave!"
Dad: (mumbling to himself) "Fine! One less lazy bum to feed."

Sadly, my experience as a clinician is that all too often what starts out as a simple question ends up in a bitter dispute, so that what should have been a discussion regarding curfew ends up being a struggle over power. The real tragedy of the above scene is not the fact that this youth and his father had incompatible goals nor that conflict resulted, but that the point of conflict moved from one of curfew to one of person. Both father and son ended the interchange feeling unloved and perhaps quite unloving.

In the process of escalation, not only do energies and employed force go beyond the level needed for resolving the initial conflict, but quite often the original issue gets lost in the heat of the exchange. The emotions peak to a point where it is not merely a problem to be resolved, but an all-out attack and counter-attack between those involved. From this perspective, resolution is not the goal; inflicting pain and destruction is.

Under a condition of such escalation both parties feel dissatisfied with the eventual outcome. Further the impact on the individual (i.e., feel inadequate, guilty, unloved, etc.) and the relationship (i.e., something to avoid) far outweighs the gains accrued for either individual. We need to avoid such escalation by learning to recognize our own emotional upset and loss of perspective. In addition to recognizing the escalation we need to learn to call a "time-out" in our discussions in order to regain a proper perspective and reduce the emotional intensity. One strategy which I have found useful for achieving this "time-out" is to have both parents and adolescents identify a "cue" or "signal" to be used when they feel that either one of them is losing perspective and that the conflict is escalating to a point of explosion. Signals such as saying "Time-out" or gesturing with one's hands as one might in a sporting event to signal time-out are useful in this situation. Regardless of the signal to be used, getting distance from the conflict is essential in order to bring the conflict back into a proper perspective and within a manageable level of intensity.

Coercion: Might Makes Right

The final pitfall which we need to be especially aware of is the tendency for one in a conflict to run to a position of power. Often when in conflict we may find ourselves attempting to coerce our youth to succumb to our demands. We may employ threats of reprisal ("you'll be sorry"), fear of punishment ("one more comment from you and you're grounded!") or guilt ("I said so and I'm your parent!") in order to resolve the conflict. Such coercion may win the battle but destroy the relationship.

When we find ourselves relying on the "mighty sword" in order to end the conflict we need to stop and ask ourselves, "At what cost is this conflict to be resolved?" The reliance on force needs to be our signal that what is merely a problem to be resolved has become a personal battle. The presence of coercion needs to signal that an opportunity for collaboration and cooperation between ourselves and our youth has now taken on adversarial features. Under these conditions we need to stop the conflict in mid-stream, remove ourself from the negative emotional climate and regain our problem solving perspective.

RESOLVING CONFLICT—A WIN-WIN STRATEGY

A "no-lose" or "win-win" approach to conflict resolution is one strategy we can employ in order to constructively resolve the conflicts we experience with our youth. The approach is one of mutual and collaborative problem solving. It requires that we and our teen be willing to sit down and move through a series of steps which should take us from problem identification through mutual resolution. Specifically this approach requires that we (1) identify our needs, (2) generate solutions, (3) evaluate, and (4) select our strategy.

Need Identification

Quite often the source of the conflict rests not in our incompatible goals or the actual blocking of goal achievement but in our own inability to identify what our goals truly are and to creatively strategize about goal achievement. For example, the girl who wishes to stay out with her friends until midnight and whose parents desire to have her safe at home by 11 P.M. may feel that their goals are incompatible and that her parents are directly interfering with her own goal achievement. Similarly, her parents may view their daughter's request to stay out until midnight as incompatible with their own need for sleep and comfort in knowing that she is home safe. Ironically, often what is perceived as incompatible is not. As such what becomes the basis of conflict can oftentimes be avoided if a parent and youth can learn to identify and articulate their real needs and find a creative way to generate possible solutions for need satisfaction. Thus in the previous example, if one were to suggest that a solution may be for both parties to give a little and compromise with 11:30 P.M. curfew, we would fail to address the real needs which are independent of the actual time of curfew. For the girl the goal is not so much a time but the need to feel as though she is trusted and that she can avoid being embarrassed in front of her friends. Her parents, on the other hand, are less concerned about the hour and more interested in her safety. If it were possible to identify these needs, we might find that there are ways for which her parents' goal of insuring her safety are achieved without embarrassing their daughter. Thus the first step in resolving conflict is for parents and their adolescent to identify and clearly state what it is that they specifically need or want. It is important to distinguish *what* we want from *how* we want to achieve it. If we remember that the time of 11 o'clock was *one* strategy for reaching our goal, we may be open to searching for other more mutually acceptable strategies for achieving our goals.

Generating Solutions/Strategies

After we have identified what it is which both parties hope to gain we begin the second step of constructive conflict resolution, generating solutions. During this step I have found it helpful to use a process such as *brainstorming.*

Brainstorming is an activity where we attempt to generate as many solutions as possible for the existing problem. During this phase the solutions do not even need to be feasible. What we are looking for is quantity of solutions. Quality will be assessed in a later step. As you begin to generate solutions you should write them down without any verbal evaluation or criticism. This point is critical and yet it is often quite difficult to achieve. If we begin to criticize one another's ideas or suggestions we may get distracted from our task, or find that we resist offering other suggestions. Thus it is essential to set as a rule: No criticism. The goal is to be creative. Often even what initially appeared as a ludicrous idea may prove to be quite productive and useful.

Evaluating the Strategies

Once a list of potential strategies is generated we need to return to each idea and begin the process of evaluating each for usefulness. During this step we need to invite our teens to identify along with us the costs and payoffs for each of the strategies listed. In this situation we are looking for the benefits gained by them or others, the problems caused for them or others, the feelings that could be aroused with this solution, and any other consequence which may result from selection of this particular solution. These costs and payoffs should be listed for each of the strategies.

Selection and Implementation

Once each of the alternatives has been analyzed for consequences and the alternatives have been rated for degree of satisfaction, one of the strategies will be decided upon and selected. Even though a strategy has been selected it is useful for both parent and teen to plan on assessing the success of the strategy selected and to discuss the pro's and con's of the process of working together in conflict resolution.

When Results Are Less Than Ideal

Using this process requires a lot of time and energy on the part of both parents and teens. Further, this approach assumes that mutual satisfaction is possible and that one of the solutions generated will be enthusiastically accepted by all parties involved. As we know from experience such mutual satisfaction is not always the case.

In those situations where no mutually satisfying solution is found, we must, as parents, take the responsibility for selecting one solution which appears to be most generally satisfying to all involved. Under these conditions our teens will be unhappy and may protest. In responding to these protests we need to alert our youth to the fact that we (parents and teens) did our best and yet fell short of finding the perfect solution. Further we need to demonstrate to our teens that we are open to considering other solutions which would move us closer to *mutual* satisfaction, should they be able to generate such solutions. But our youth need to be reminded that at the current time the solution selected is the best of all that *we* were able to generate.

The frustration of not getting what we want is part of the human condition. Our adolescents, like us, will be unhappy and disappointed at the failure to find a totally satisfying solution. However, the process of attempting to work together should help them appreciate that we care about them and respect their needs and as such may help to make the frustration a bit more palatable. Thus even when time and energy are limited or where the nature of the conflicting needs is such that mutual satisfaction is not possible, using the no-lose process can be an effective way of demonstrating our concern and willingness to work with our teens.

Parent Points

- Conflict is inevitable—but not inevitably destructive.
- Creative, constructive resolution to conflict can result in increased communication and understanding between parent and teen.
- Constructive resolution requires:
  **appreciation for the legitimacy of our youths' needs;
  **the avoidance of a "might makes right" orientation;
  **a non-escalating, rational problem solving approach.
- Keep perspective—conflict is of point, not of person.
- When emotions blur vision and problem solving, take *time-out.*
- Distinguish *what* I want from *how* I want to get it.
- Recognize that there is more than one path or one strategy to need satisfaction.
- See conflict as an invitation to grow in love and understanding through mutual problem solving.

6.

Sex—A Matter of Do's, Not Don'ts

Don't touch this or that! Don't look at this or listen to that! And never but never think about doing that! Yeah, I know all the don'ts*—but what are the* Do's*?*

(Tom, age 16)

Christmas 1986 marked the inauguration of a new Parsons' family tradition. Following upon the guidance and modeling of comedian-actor Bill Cosby, my wife and I proudly presented our fifteen year old son, Kristian, the "official" Parsons razor and shaving cream. This tradition was certainly not novel, nor was it necessarily our son's official rite of passage into manhood. It was, however, one way that two anxious parents could let their son know of their awareness of his sexual maturation.

Sexual maturation are two words which most parents of teens dread. The sound of those words often conjures up images of teens asking embarrassing questions, parents discovering their youth in compromising positions, or the terrifying possibility of our children becoming parents with out-of-wedlock pregnancies. We are anxious and confused about what to say or what to do. We may even attempt to overlook or ignore the natural signs of our adolescent's ongoing sexual maturation. It is as if we wish to pretend that our children are just that, children, and have not entered the realm of the sexually mature. Despite our own anxieties about our youths' sexual maturation, it is inevitable. Our teens are becoming sexually mature, and it will become quite apparent to them, to us, and to the rest of the world. Just as inevitable are the questions, concerns and interests our teenagers will have about their sexual changes. As with so many other wonderful events in their life our teens need us to serve as a source of information and support during this time of their sexual maturation.

The Announcement

Like myself and my wife, some parents recognize their youths' deeper voice, changing physiques or increased hair as announcements of their emerging maturity and sexuality. Other parents are brought into the awareness of their teens' sexual development through a more blatant announcement. Perhaps they discover their teens engaged in sexual activity. They may discover a pornographic magazine or contraceptive device in their youths' rooms or notice the effects of their sexual activity (e.g., a "hickey" or even pregnancy). Whether it be through our perception of our youths' increased physical maturity or our discovery of their sexual interest and activity, the *announcement* of their sexual maturation will be made.

Adolescence is by definition that period of development initiated with the growth of primary and secondary sex characteristics. While adolescence is not the first nor the last time one's sexuality will be examined and explored, it is a very special time. It is a time involving much more than simply the growth of the adolescents' sex organs or the stimulation and arousal of sex hormones and the drive toward intimacy. The period of adolescence is a time for our adolescents to begin to make a number of personal, value based decisions regarding *relationship, intimacy* and their own *sexual identity*. It is a time of great confusion and concern for adolescents.

As such, the "announcement" of our youths' sexual maturation brings with it an R.S.V.P. to parents. Our children have many unanswered questions and concerns and they seek and need both wisdom and counsel. As parents, our children's entry into sexual maturity is therefore an invitation for us to respond with support and guidance. As previously suggested, however, this invitation often causes parents much anxiety and consternation. "I don't know what to tell him; let the school do it" is a response which many of us feel, if not actually state. And while we may attempt to ignore the changes impacting on our teens we cannot simply wish away the inevitable events which accompany their sexual maturation.

The Need for Response

Phrases such as "I don't know what to say" or "Go ask your mother (or father)," point quite clearly to our own need for wisdom and counsel. While we may appreciate the need for having something said to our youth, we may feel that the time is not right, or that we are not well enough prepared to have that special talk. The response which our adolescents require is not "the special talk." Rather they are wondering how we survived the many concerns of adolescence. They wish to know how we have resolved the various conflicts and issues of sexuality which they need to address. They need us to respond with our availability, our willingness to listen and our loving support.

As parents we need to be awakened to the nature of our adolescents' sexual development and the role we play in their sexual education. One's sexuality is a special gift of life that requires particular understanding and responsible decision making. We need to assist our teens to understand the beauty and mystery of this gift of sexuality. Further, we need to help them to develop the knowledge and strength required to respond to this gift in a way which will facilitate their own personal, spiritual growth.

It is not acceptable to simply assume that our teens will know what is right and do what they should. Nor can we abdicate our role as primary educators and assume that the schools or the Church will educate them to respond to their sexuality. The statistics on adolescent pregnancy, venereal disease, AIDS, abortion and promiscuity show the necessity of value-based guidance and direction in matters of sexuality. Such guidance and direction start at home!

The statistics tell only part of the story. My own experience with teens and the research of others point to the fact that most adolescents *want* to discuss the sexual dimension of their life with their parents. Yet for most parents the area of their teens' sexuality remains shrouded in myth, mystery, fear and confusion. It is often a topic to be avoided rather than one to be embraced.

Responding with Information

Most teens find the new experiences and sensations which accompany their sexual awakening to be quite disconcerting and confusing. So it is not very surprising to find that they will jump at the chance to ask questions or share experiences. Whether it be under the cover of anonymity as they turn in a written question to their religion or biology teacher, or in the privacy of a counselor's office, or while watching TV with mom and dad, teens want and need information about their emerging sexuality. The sexually maturing adolescents need answers and honest information regarding their bodies, the process and experience of sexual activity, and areas of special concern such as homosexuality, masturbation, and venereal disease.

When their questions go unanswered by someone with accurate, value-based information our teens will turn to other sources for answers (peers, pornographic literature, or even trial and error learning). The result of such "street learning" is both misinformation and all too often misfortune!

As parents we may exclaim that we are not experts and that we don't completely understand our own physiology much less that of our teens. However, we don't have to be experts to provide our sons and daughters with the information they seek. Much of what we take as common knowledge, information that we have come to understand through our own struggles and experience, is that which is sought by our youth. Our teenage son's concerns over what appears to be uncontrollable erections or nocturnal ejaculations (wet dreams) are experiences he shares in common with his father. Similarly, the adolescents' interest in the pain or pleasure associated with intercourse or the meaning of certain terms such as "french kissing" are almost certainly within a parent's realm of expertise. There are clearly questions and concerns for which you and I are not prepared to provide the information requested. And while it is important to be informed, we need not have, or expect ourselves to have, all of the answers. It is O.K. to admit to not having all the answers. It is even O.K. to admit to being uncomfortable and nervous about our discussions. But it is *not* O.K. to allow these feelings to be our excuse for avoiding dialogue with our teens. Our willingness, interest and availability to share with our youth are more important than our absolute expertise.

Our children are most likely filled with many questions and curiosities. It is important that we learn to understand their questions and respond to them as they were intended, directly and honestly. Quite often our own anxieties force us to read into the question, imagining it to mean or imply much more than it does. Most of us, for example, have laughed at the story of the father who nearly passed out when asked by his four year old: "Daddy, where did I come from?" Thoughts of "go ask your mother" and "where is that Spock book?" ran through the man's mind as he attempted to formulate his father-son presentation. Of course it was his own anxiety to which the man responded, since the child only wished to know whether it was Cleveland or Columbus! Learning to hear past our own hang-ups and anxieties is essential if we are to provide our youth with the information and counsel they seek. One technique I have found helpful in this matter is to reflect questions back to teens and ask how they see it or what they think about the issue. The way they answer our question may provide us with greater insight into what it is they are really seeking. Along this line, I can remember one fifteen year old girl who asked me whether losing one's virginity was painful. My first inclination was to assume she was thinking about the pain reported to be associated with breaking a female's hymen. Luckily, I decided to follow my own advice and asked her for her opinion. Surprisingly what followed was a discussion not of physiology but of philosophy and psychology. Her concern was not one of physical pain, but of the pain one might experience in losing childhood innocence and moving toward emotional intimacy that accompanied moving from childhood (her virginity) to adulthood (and sexual intimacy).

In addition to learning to hear what is being asked, we need to become sensitive to *how* it is asked. Most teens are struggling with their sexuality—a struggle which is often exhibited in their embarrassment or difficulty in expressing themselves. They are sensitive, anxious and confused. We need to be sensitive to their confusions and anxieties. What may first appear to be something silly or insignificant may be an issue of crisis proportion for them. As such we need to avoid criticism or sarcastic humor in responding. We need to respect their curiosity, their concern and their quest for guidance. We need to convey to them that they are not alone. Their questions and concerns are normal and experienced by us all. As such it is helpful for our children to understand that we too have had questions and concerns about our sexuality. Further, they need to hear that, like them, we have found comfort in sharing these with people we love.

Responding with Values: The "Do's" Rather Than the "Don'ts"

Sex education is more than facts and figures. As Christian parents educating the total person, we need to assist our youth to understand the emotions, values and responsibilities which guide their use of these facts and figures.

Our teens need counsel which will not only provide them with accurate information but will also help them to make the appropriate decisions that will lead them to a fuller appreciation of the gift of sexuality with which the Creator has endowed them. They are in need of a clear sense and vision of Christian sexuality and its implications for mature and appropriate conditions of intimacy.

Historically, parents have played the role of enforcer of the *don'ts.* Techniques ranging from the use of a chastity belt (or its modern day equivalent of the ever-present, overprotective and restrictive parent as escort) through the use of guilt and fear have been employed in our effort to prevent sexual interest and action among our teens. Our experience shows us that reliance on "the don'ts" does not work. The statistics of increased promiscuity, teen pregnancies and venereal disease demonstrate the ineffectiveness of such preventive methods. In fact the use of such preventive approaches may even increase our youth's interest and desire for the "forbidden fruit."

In addition to the ineffectiveness of this approach, quite often the employment of fear and guilt as preventive techniques prove damaging and destructive to the individual. More than one individual has been psychologically and emotionally scarred and spiritually disenfranchised because of the darkness of ingrained guilt. Too many adults are unable to rejoice in their sexuality because of their ignorance or guilt about being sexual. Similarly, too many individuals have been separated from their religion because of guilt surrounding their previous sexual actions. Such psycho-emotional and spiritual damage in combination with the statistics of increased adolescent sexual activity points to the need to move away from our education of *don'ts* to an education of *do's.* Do rejoice in one's sexuality! Do see one's sexuality as encompassing more than one's genitals! Do view sexuality as an expression of Christ's loving relationship with us! Do use Christ as our model of intimacy!

Do Rejoice. We need to encourage our sons and daughters to appreciate and to enjoy their sexuality. *Do* rejoice in being sexual. It is essential that we instill in our youth the appreciation of their sexuality as truly a special gift of life. It is a gift which allows us to participate in the creative love of God, living in communion with him through another. It is a gift of oneness, a gift of intimacy and completedness. However, for many men and women sexuality has been reduced to a genital experience. We need to assist our youth to appreciate sexuality as a vocation between men and women to become whole in relationship, in love.

Do See Sex As More Than Genital. It is important to help our teens expand their view of sexuality beyond that of genital contact. We need to help them come to appreciate that constant involvement in self-indulgent sexual practices is contrary to the mature expression of one's sexuality, and that while sexuality involves self, it is more fully realized in terms of self in relationship to others. Our youth need to begin to recognize the beauty of their sexuality in that it highlights their desire and ability to be intimate. Sexuality is evidence of our ability to share in a loving relationship and to exchange the mutual gift of self. It is important that we (they) *do* view sex as relational, not as merely genital. With an expanded view, our youth can appreciate that sexuality in the teen years is not only the *dont's,* but includes the *do's* of *sharing* and *caring* for one another. Coming to share and experience the love of friendship is an essential part of being human and an active element to their sexuality. Adolescence is a special time of sexuality. It is a time when the closeness and intimacy of a special friend can be experienced—the intimacy and oneness of sharing their pain and disappointments with a friend or partaking in the joy of another. These, too, are essential elements in the total sexual experience. We need to help our sons and daughters to recognize that these experiences like those physical accompaniments are all part of the gift of sexuality God has provided—a gift which represents total self-giving in a covenant relationship.

Do View Sexuality as an Expression of Christ's Loving Relationship with Us. We need to convey to our children that it is important that they *do* view their sexuality as an opportunity for unselfish love—a love to which we are all called by Christ to share, a love for which Christ has proven the perfect model. It is important to invite our youth to consider Christ as their model of intimacy, a model to be used to guide their own value based decisions. For example, it may be helpful to have our teens who are faced with the dilemma of engaging in premarital intercourse to contrast their "loving relationship" with that modeled by Christ. With Jesus as their model of intimacy they can begin to question whether this relationship, this partner with whom they wish to become intimate, is an open friendship (John 14:14). Do they see the relationship as reflecting a faithfulness to self and to the other (John 14:18)? Do they see the relationship as one reflecting an appropriate willingness for self-sacrifice (John 15:13)? With such questions in mind our teens may recognize that this or that relationship is less than mutual and clearly not unselfish. They may appreciate that the push toward sexual intimacy is driven by self-centeredness. Often such an awareness will provide the basis from which a mature, responsible, value-based decision can be made.

New Wonders, New Worries, New Opportunities

Our teens' sexual awakening is both a wonderful and a disconcerting event. For the teens new experiences are often exciting yet anxiety provoking. Questions around the what, the why, and the how of things that are being experienced make this a time during which our adolescent will seek and need much wisdom and counsel. It is also a time of excitement and anxiety for parents. For us, the parents, our concerns over our youth's ability to know and do what is right and to avoid the dangers of immature and irresponsible sexuality often blind us to the joy and beauty of this latest stage in our children's development.

Our teens want and need to hear how we have worked out our own answers to the many questions of sexuality with which they are engaged. Learning to hear their questions and respond openly and honestly is yet another opportunity for us to grow together. Our availability to them throughout this time of concern and our willingness to share honestly and genuinely will provide the foundations from which they will develop their own sense of sexuality and sexual responsibility.

We are made in the image of God, and in our sexuality we give witness to the love from which our own desire to love springs forth.

Parent Points

- **Being human is being sexual.**
- **Sexuality is a gift, to be valued, to be used responsibly.**
- **As sex educators, it is O.K. for us to be anxious and even less than expert. It is not O.K. to use this as our excuse for not performing our roles as teachers.**
- **Our youth are in need of information (wisdom) and guidance (counsel). Together we should seek accurate information and avoid rigid, personal proselytizing.**
- **Our teens want to share their experiences, their concerns and their questions. We need to be sensitive and available to their concerns.**
- **In responding to our youth's concerns we need to go beyond facts and figures. We need to share our values and vision. Similarly, we need to keep in mind our own personal story of struggle and resolution. Our children want to know how we have resolved these issues.**
- **We need to help our youth be guided in their decisions by a set of *do's* rather than *don'ts.***
  ****Do see sexuality as more than genital, as relational.**
  ****Do desire to be caring and loving, and seek intimate loving relationships.**
  ****Do use Christ as our model of intimacy, seeking relationships which are open, true to our values, and involving appropriate mutual self-sacrifice.**

****Do view our sexuality in light of God's love and Christ's invitation to "come, follow me."**

****Do develop a warm, affective sense of God's love in our sexuality.**

7.

Drugs: Just Say No!

Yeah, I'm high on life. I just need a snort now and then to keep me that way.

(Maria, age 13)

Saying yes to life and no to drug and alcohol use is not easy for the adolescent of the 1980's. Crack, pot, smack, and the more exotic "designer" drugs can be found in any community and any school. We live in a culture where our models, our heroes, often present drugs and alcohol as the key to relaxing or the means of making it. Messages such as "drinking is cool," "getting high is O.K." and popping or snorting this or that is "what everybody's doing" bombard our teens from every corner of their lives. TV, music, peers and even parents invite teens to just get high! And while we may be shocked or surprised by Maria's comment (after all, she is only thirteen), the sad truth is that Maria is far from being alone among her peers.

Opening up our morning paper we are bound to see a story of a neighborhood youth involved in some drug related incident. Alcohol and drug usage among our teens is at epidemic proportions, and as parents we cannot bury our heads, claiming that it's not happening to our kids. Good kids, good families and good schools are not insurance against drug and alcohol abuse.

Like many parents of teenagers I am concerned. I am concerned that my children may not really understand the effects, the dangers of using drugs or alcohol. I am concerned that even if they do, they will find it hard to resist the temptation, the pressure, to at least try them. I am concerned that I may not know how to respond in order to help my children navigate through these very threatening times and serious decisions.

Each of us needs to become knowledgeable about the "what's" and the "what to do's" of teenage drug use. We need to learn to discern curiosity from crisis. We need to discern a use from an abuse. We need to learn how, as well as how not, to react to our children involved with drugs or alcohol. The current chapter will address these many concerns of parents of teenagers who like myself hope and pray they will say *No*.

Times Have Changed

If you and I could search back to our own teenage years we might discover that for most of us it was a time of experimentation, a time when we tried on many varied hats and when we tried to act like those much older than ourselves. Often our experimentation and desire to act older may have taken us behind the garage or down at the corner where we choked through our first cigarette. Or perhaps some of us experimented by sneaking drinks at a family outing or grabbing one of mom and dad's beers before going to the dance. Adolescence as a period of development has a long-standing history of such experimentation. This experimentation, along with the desire to be older, serves as a primary reason for many teens' involvement with drugs and alcohol.

Today's youth, like those of previous generations, will experiment. Many of the statistics suggest that niney-five percent of all youth will have tried smoking marijuana or drinking alcohol before the age of seventeen. Unlike previous generations our teens have many new and more dangerous ways of experimentation. For many teens acquiring marijuana, amphetamines, barbiturates or even cocaine is as easy as sneaking that cigarette or grabbing that beer. The game looks the same but the rules and the costs of playing are much greater. Teens today are no longer just risking getting caught and punished by mom and dad. Today's teenagers who experiment with drugs find that they are gambling with physical damage, dependency, and death.

The "What"

If we are to assist our youth in understanding the potential implications for their experimentation, we must become informed. A complete description of the various types of drugs and their effects is beyond the scope of this chapter. It is suggested, therefore, that you contact your local school guidance department or health agency for informational pamphlets and fact sheets regarding drugs and their effects. Of the many drugs available to our teens, alcohol and marijuana remain the drugs of choice. As such they are discussed in some detail.

Alcohol. Regardless of what the law is, or what we as parents proclaim, the simple fact is that many teenagers drink and far too many die as a result of that drinking. Drunk (or drugged) driving is America's leading killer of teenagers. It has been estimated that as many as fifty thousand young people die or suffer serious injury as a result of drinking and driving. Drinking can't be controlled by rules or prohibition; our national history shows us that! Our teens will have to make their own decisions about drinking. Therefore our role must be one of providing information which will help them to understand both the negatives of alcohol as well as the positives of responsible drinking.

First of all we all must understand that alcohol *is a drug*. Many parents feel relieved in discovering that their child, who appears drugged or stoned, is *only* drunk. Such an attitude supports our young people's drinking. It is as if we are publicly saying: Don't do drugs, but it's O.K. to drink. Alcohol is a drug—no if, ands, or buts about it!

While most people think it is a stimulant, alcohol is actually a depressant. It is a general anesthetic which causes depression of the central nervous system. The experience of being high is really a result of the alcohol reducing the brain's control over behavior. Its depressant effect results in gradual loss of control over certain cognitive and motor functions. As the amount of alcohol in the bloodstream increases, vision becomes impaired, depth perception distorted, speech thickened and slurred. Coordination deteriorates. Many teenagers believe they can will themselves through the effects of alcohol. The reality is that regardless of what they think they can do, drunkenness is a state of physical and mental incompetence. If enough alcohol is consumed, drowsiness, sleep or even death will result.

While nothing will keep alcohol from having its effects, eating before and while drinking will slow down the rate of absorption and thus slow down the effects of alcohol somewhat. But our teens need to understand that regardless of whether they eat or not, drinking too much will make them drunk.

Marijuana. Marijuana is the dried flowers, leaves and stems of the plant *Cannabis sativa.* It can be ingested or smoked. The plant has four hundred substances which convert to over two thousand chemical compounds, including delta-9-tetrahydrocannabinol (THC), the most psychoactive or mind-altering of its compounds. Unlike alcohol, THC is not water soluble; hence it does not clear from the body easily. Instead it tends to seek out and seep into fatty sections of cells and fatty organs. It can take up to four weeks for the THC in a single marijuana cigarette to clear from the body.

Marijuana changes one's sensory perception and often provides an individual with a dreamy state of relaxation. While the ill-effects of short-term, low-dosage use are neither clear nor generally agreed upon, most researchers will warn of the subsequent secondary dangers (for example, driving a car) which occur as a result of the slower reaction time, distorted perception and unrealistic feelings of well-being. Research on long-term, chronic use suggests that marijuana smoking leads to lung damage, a depression of the immune system, an altering of the balance of the adolescent sex hormones, and possible long-term memory loss. In addition to such physical effects, marijuana has been associated with other social and psychological effects. Adolescents who smoke marijuana are often reported to exhibit energy loss, diminished school performance, low motivation, and low self-esteem.

The "What to Do"

As with so many other dangers which have confronted my children I sometimes wish I could just will the problem away. But willing the problem away will not work, and ignoring it is sure to invite its presence. Drug and alcohol use among teens scares me, and I am sure it scares you. We do not have to surrender to our fear, however. There are a number of steps which we can take. Although these steps are not foolproof, they may help reduce the chances that our youth will develop a drug or alcohol problem.

Drug Free Stance. Too many parents fear seeming "uncool" or not with it if they take a stance against teenage drinking or drug use. I have had interaction with more than one parent who overlooked their teen's use of a "little marijuana" or taking a "couple of drinks." Many parents directly support their children's use of drugs by offering alcohol at home parties. Others, while not directly offering alcohol or drugs to their teens, may directly support it by overlooking the evidence that such drinking and marijuana smoking is going on within their homes. We must give substance to our verbal convictions. We need to "say *No*" to our teens' use of drugs and alcohol inside the home as well as out.

In addition to asserting our own stance against drug and alcohol use by our teens at home, we need to assess our own use of drugs and alcohol. We need to consider the standards we are modeling. We need to question whether or not we are modeling responsible use of alcohol.

Further many parents with whom I have worked suggest the value of contacting and working with the parents of their adolescent's friends. One community for example developed a collective stance against drugs. They signed a contract stating that they would only allow their children to attend parties which were supervised and drug and alcohol free. Further they each agreed to supervise all teen parties and gatherings and prohibit the use of drugs or alcohol within their homes. This sign of solidarity not only reinforces the standards for their teens but helps to remove some of the opportunity and peer pressure those teens may experience. As Tom (age 16) noted: "It's not such an embarrassment to have a party where there is no drinking or doing dope. After all, everybody has the same rules!"

For some parents it may already be clear that their teens are frequent users of drugs and alcohol. When it is clear that teens are engaged in regular use of drugs, parents must take the stance that they must stop *completely* and *immediately*. If the teens resist or are uncooperative, parents must be prepared to seek professional assistance. They cannot let fear of "what the neighbors may say" stand in their way. Fear and embarrassment are not the issue; the health and well being of their teens is!

Share Facts Not Fiction. While we need to be sure not to underplay the effect of drug and alcohol use, we must not assume effects that are not likely. Too often parents, in their attempt to prevent their teens from experimenting with drugs and alcohol, use scare tactics.

I can remember one parent who was frantic and visibly quite upset as he described finding a small aspirin case filled with marijuana in his son's jeans. The father was armed with articles and leaflets and was asking whether I thought his son needed to be hospitalized. When I asked the father a few questions about his son's behavior and any previous evidence or experience with drugs or alcohol it became clear that hospitalization was unneeded. However, the father was unhappy with my apparent carefree attitude. He began to berate the youth, noting that "everyone knows that marijuana is addicting and leads people to become heroin addicts!"

While a case may be made that involvement with one type of drug makes one more vulnerable to experimentation with other forms of drugs, such a definite cause–effect relationship between infrequent use of marijuana and eventual heroin addiction is unsupported.

Parents may be tempted to prevent their teens' experimentation with drugs and alcohol by depicting horrible and extreme consequences of drug use. Such tactics not only fail to inhibit teens experimentation but actually may prove counter-productive. Teens are somewhat knowledgeable about the effects of many drugs. Thus, when they hear a parent incorrectly condemning marijuana because "it causes a person to become a heroin addict," they may not only reject this point but all other points raised by the parent.

Our teens need accurate information about the types of drugs currently popular and the *known* long and short term effects of each. Although most schools have incorporated drug education into their curriculum, such education needs to be reinforced at home.

In discussing drug usage with teens we need to be armed with facts. We need to be familiar with the effects that the various types of drugs can have on the physical, social and emotional well-being of the users. We need to talk about the undesirable behavioral changes and health problems which accompany such drug use. We need to talk about the positive aspects of non-use.

Keep the Lines of Communication Open. In addition to becoming informed and knowledgeable, we should develop and maintain open lines of communication with our teens. Open discussions about the prevalence of drugs, their effects and the problems they cause will provide the basis for healthy decision making.

In order for us to have such dialogue we must be willing to listen to our teens, *calmly and caringly.* We need to avoid overreacting to the information presented even when some of the information may surprise or shock us. The parents who threaten to kill their child or ground them forever if they ever take a drink or smoke a joint are inviting that child to become very secretive and non-communicative.

Our teens must learn to act responsibly. If we are to assist them, then it is imperative that we listen to what they are experiencing. We need to understand the role that drugs play in their society and convey to them our real understanding of the stress and pressure they face.

Teach Our Teens How To Say *No.* In addition to listening we need to provide our teens with ammunition which they can use to resist the peer pressure they may face. It may seem simple to say to them, "Just say *no,*" but the pressure to conform, the pressure to try, is sometimes hard to resist. This is especially true of teens who feel that they desperately need to be accepted by their peers and fear that such acceptance may be jeopardized if they say no to drug or alcohol use.

If we simply and somewhat rigidly tell our teens "Don't worry; who needs those types of friends anyway?" then we have probably failed to appreciate the real pressure they are experiencing. We need to help them develop strategies for avoiding and resisting this pressure.

Teaching teens to say no in ways which will not threaten their standing with peers will prove quite helpful. One technique which I have found useful is to have both parents and teens present sample scenarios and ask each to respond to the situation in a way that may save face yet still say no. For example, we might ask teens to consider how they might respond in the situation where a friend invites them over to discuss a serious problem that he is experiencing with his girl friend. As they are talking, the friend lights up a joint just to relax and passes it on to them to share. The question is: How do they say no, yet maintain their friendship? A second example may further help to illustrate the type of dilemmas posed for discussion: "Consider how you might respond to the situation where you are at a party. The parents of the teen who is having the party step out and one of the kids at the party starts to pass around quarts of beer. A quart is handed to you, and it is your turn to chug. How do you respond?"

While it would be nice to believe that our teens will have the strength of conviction to simply stand their ground and say no, sometimes they need help. Having the facts to back up their stand will help, but their resistance can be made easier if they are familiar with face-saving strategies, such as "parents as excuse," "friendship pact" and "escape techniques."

For example we may give our teen permission to use us as an excuse. I can remember one teen, Tom, who found it difficult to say *no* to his friends when they attempted to buy and drink beer when he was driving. Tom had no real desire to drink but found it hard to ask his friends not to drink in his car. After explaining his dilemma to his father, his dad simply suggested that he use his dad as his excuse. Tom's father suggested that Tom tell his friends that his father had a nose of a bloodhound and that he would take away the car forever if he smelled beer in it. Tom only used the excuse once but all the guys understood. Since it was more important to keep their one ride available (Tom had the only car in the group) they freely gave up the drinking in order to keep the wheels!

In addition to using parents as excuse, many teens find that it helps if they can form a drug-free pact with at least one other friend. Linda, age sixteen, found it easy to say no to invitations to drink or smoke dope, knowing that if she said no, Kathy, her best friend, would also decline. Knowing that she would not be isolated or alone, and that at least two people at the party would not be doing drugs, provided Linda the emotional support she needed to stand up to the peer pressure.

Finally, teaching our youth a variety of escape techniques such as humor (*No* thanks; I'm naturally stoned!) or delay tactics (Maybe later; I feel a bit sick, or not now; I'm just not into it) will also prove helpful in learning to deal with the social pressures they experience.

While our goal as parents is not to simply provide our youth with tricks and strategies to avoid social pressure, such avoidance and immediate problem solving will provide the foundation from which to continue to develop our parent-teen relationship. As the relationship continues to grow and we can shift our discussion from that of drugs and alcohol to that of peers, friendship and social pressure, we will also be able to help our youth develop a stronger self-concept and an assertive orientation. It is this firm self-concept which will provide the basis from which our teen will be able to simply say no without need for further excuse or justification.

Provide Alternatives. In addition to assisting our youth to say no, we need to provide them with opportunities to socialize in safe, drug free environments. We need to be willing to host our teens' parties or provide them with recreational outlets (which may mean driving here or there). We may need to become more active in our schools, our churches and our communities. As active church and community members we may be able to develop opportunities for our teens to socialize and engage in recreation in the drug free environments. Many churches currently provide teens with meeting places (such as a teen club), supervised dances, talent nights, rap groups, etc. Further, our church could and should provide the arena for the establishment of youth groups and supervised sports and recreational outings. We need to work together to establish common rules for our children that make drugs and alcohol off-limits, but we also need to help them find healthy alternatives.

Parent Points

- Ours is a drug culture. Getting high is promoted by athletes, rock stars, and many others in the public eye.

- Good kids from good families and in good schools *do* get high!

- The reasons for teenage drinking and doing drugs are many:
  **To fit in: "everybody does it!"
  **To follow a role model, including a parent!
  **To escape from the pain of family or the trials of adolescence.
  **To experiment, just to see what it is like.

- Our youth need help to say *no.*

- As parents we can help if
  **We listen and appreciate the pressures they confront.
  **We respond with facts, not fiction. We must not overplay the dangers of drugs nor should we underplay them!
  **We teach our teens how to say *no.*
  **If we model responsible decision making and say *no* to teen drinking and drug use.

8.

Peers: Help or Hindrance?

I know, I know. "People who need people are the luckiest people. . ." It's O.K. that my son needs *people, needs his friends but why does he have to* need *such bums!"*

Relationships, intimacy, and belonging are characteristic needs of all human beings. We are social by nature; we seek relationship!

There is probably no other time in our developmental stages when this need, this interest, this drive to belong is so clear than is it during adolescence. Adolescents spend a great deal of time and energy being with their peers.

"I have to call Danny!" (even though I just left him ten minutes ago at school)

"Look, I'll walk. It's only one mile and everybody is going to be there!" (Even though I wouldn't walk a block down to the store to get my mom milk).

"If I don't get invited, I'll just die!" (Well, not die, but it would be horrible!)

Peers! Sometimes you can't live with them, but who wants to live without them! Some of our teens' happiest and most fulfilling moments, as well as some of their greatest hurts and frustrations, will come at the hands of their peers. Similarly, many of our own parenting frustrations will come as a result of our teens' involvement with peers.

The current chapter discusses the role and value of peers to our teens' development. Understanding the value served by their friends will assist us in guiding them so that peers will be a help and not a hindrance to their own development.

The Need

Adolescents are struggling between two very important life tasks. They are seeking to identify who they are and who they are to become. At the same time, they are beginning to feel the need and desire to share this newly found identity with another. The tasks of establishing one's self-identity and moving toward intimacy require that our youth become part of a peer society.

Peers serve a number of very important functions. First, our teens' peers offer an arena for learning and developing new skills, new attitudes and new roles. By watching their peers, teens begin to learn how to dress, how to dance, how to argue, how to be cool and uncool, and simply how to be in this new society.

In addition, the peer group provides the opportunity to practice many new-found behaviors. Being sexual, learning to date and interact maturely with the opposite sex, exhibiting and controlling one's anger and aggression, and simply testing new ideas are things which are essential for the development of self. However, these behaviors cannot be attempted or enacted at home with mom and dad. Our teens need peers for such skill development.

Besides simply learning and practicing new skills and attitudes, teens need and seek feedback about how they are perceived and received in the world, outside the family. Knowing that they are liked and seen as athletic, handsome, funny or nice provides them with the feedback required for developing their self-identity. Finally, the peer group provides them support and reassurance during this period of struggle. When our teens are anxious or stressed because of conflicts at home, the felt pressure from school, or the uncertainty of their future, they can find relief by expressing these concerns to an empathizing group of peers.

The peer group is certainly a valuable resource for the healthy development of our youth. However, this potentially positive resource can prove quite destructive to our teens and damaging to our relationship with them.

From Need to Needy

To many adolescents, peers are the most important aspect of their lives. These teens will go along with anything, do anything, respond in any way, just to belong. For such teens being excluded from a particular group is not merely an inconvenience or a shame, but a major catastrophe. The rejection is viewed as clear evidence that they are nothing, nobody. What's worse, often these teens view the exclusion or rejection from one group of friends as evidence of their overall unacceptability. It is as if not only does this group reject them, but no one will accept them.

Clearly, when peer groups become so essential, they can also become quite destructive. Wanting to belong so desperately invites one to be vulnerable to the negative, destructive influences of a peer group. Claire (age sixteen) was quite clear about the force and destructiveness of her desperate need to belong, but was unable to resist the strong sense of desperation.

> I know it's stupid, but you get to the point where you'll do or say anything just so you don't look like a nerd. My parents don't smoke or drink, and I don't even like it. But when I'm with my friends I just can't say no!

Another youth with whom I was working characterized the pressure and the fear of being rejected as follows.

> You have no idea what it's like. I mean, if you don't follow along they'll just dump you. You have to dress like them, do what they do, if you want to belong. Man, I couldn't imagine not being part of my group. It would be like being strung out all alone, the last person on earth, a real nerd, a loser. Who wants that!

When our teens view rejection as such a catastrophe, such an absolutely unbearable situation, they become open to extreme and potentially lethal reactions to exclusion.

> Yeah, I tried to gas myself in the car. I'll do it again! Why not? I have nothing to live for. I have no friends. Nobody ever calls

or wants me around. Nobody invites me to go with them. So what else do you want me to do?

Not all teens feel so desperately in need of peer connection. However, all teens need to seek and value peer interaction. As parents, we need to help our youth respond to the positive influence of their peers while at the same time feeling secure and assertive enough to resist the potentially damaging effects of peer pressure.

When a teen has a very poor sense of who he or she is, feels unliked and out of step with the world, that teen is quite vulnerable to the negative influences of a peer group. As parents, while we may be aware of the potential danger, we may feel helpless in terms of how to respond. Responses such as "Who needs those kids anyway? You have us!" not only fail to teach our children how to deal with peer rejection but oftentimes convey to them that we *really do not* understand the crisis they are experiencing.

If we were confronted by a friend who just lost a loved one through death or divorce we would not simply state, "Who needs that person anyway? You have us!" Yet it is this same sense of insensitivity which many teens perceive in their parents' attempts to reassure.

Rather than asking our children not to need, not to care, we need to have them solve problems with us. Problem solving requires that we, along with our teen, consider questions such as: "Why is this group (as opposed to some other) the group of choice?" or "What brings them together?" These questions will help us to identify criteria for admission into this group or the basis upon which our teens were excluded. With this knowledge perhaps we can help our teens develop a plan for gaining acceptance by the group or help them recognize that such acceptance is not worth the effort. Perhaps an example may help to further clarify the need for a "problem solving approach" to the issue of peers and peer rejection.

Tom was a fourteen year old youth who was referred to me because of his strange way of behaving and acting in school. Tom would often make funny noises, blurt out obscenities, and wear unusual clothing to school (two different shoes, gas station attendant coveralls, etc.). Our discussions made it clear that Tom found it impossible to fit in with the other kids in his class. He felt that they laughed at him, mocked him and generally thought he was a "nerd." His response to this rejection was twofold. Tom found that by dressing strangely and acting inappropriately in class, the kids would at least pay attention to him. He found that when they made fun of him he was able to feel less threatened since he could justify in his own mind that they "just didn't get into his punk style."

Initially, Tom was quite strong in stating that he didn't need them and that it was really that group who were the nerds. He would go on trying to convince me (and himself) that he "really didn't need or want any friends, especially that group. They are all weird, goody-goodies!" Eventually Tom shared that he really wished he could just be like anybody else and fit in.

Once he was willing to accept his desire to belong, he and I were able to begin problem solving. We discussed the group membership and the group's activities. We tried to identify which type of person would be included, which would be rejected and which members were really the stars of the group. On inspection it became clear that those who played key roles in the group were the kids who were knowledgeable about the latest musical groups. Also it appeared that a primary activity of the group was sharing records, tapes, posters and other information about the various musical groups. As we continued analyzing the problem Tom recognized that the kids who were generally ignored or excluded by the group were those who fought a lot or tended to get into trouble at school.

With this information in hand, Tom and I decided to do a little experiment. We decided that over the course of the next week he would slowly "tone down" his punk-like attire. It appeared that such dress was associated with the more rowdy kids. We decided that he would make small changes at first such as wearing sweat shirts to school (a common practice among the targeted group), and slowly move to changing his hair style (making it a bit less radical). Also, he would begin to demonstrate both his interest in and knowledge of music. This would be accomplished by taking in a copy of "Rolling Stone" (a music magazine) to read during free period, bringing his "Walkman" cassette player with the latest album, and most importantly allowing anyone who might be interested to borrow his materials.

In approaching the situation as a problem to be resolved, I was able to help Tom gain a degree of acceptance by the group. More importantly, however, was the fact that by analyzing the whats and the whys of the group, Tom recognized that it was *not* he who was previously rejected by the group, but the way he acted and behaved. Depersonalizing the rejection helped Tom feel much more accepting of himself. It is hoped that such self-acceptance will provide the base from which Tom will be able to be independent of group approval and be free from his previously desperate need to fit in. The knowledge that his peers may not like how he acts, or how he looks, or what he enjoys, rather than misinterpreting that it is he that they dislike, makes their criticism, their disapproval much more tolerable.

The Selection of a Group

Adolescents, like adults, select friends using a number of different criteria. As with Tom, many youth fail to understand the criteria for admission. Thus it is helpful for us as parents to understand the basis upon which a particular friend or group of friends is selected. This knowledge will not only help us to assist our teens in gaining acceptance with those they desire, but will also help us to recognize when the method of selection may be potentially harmful to our teens.

Utility. One basis upon which "friends" are sometimes selected is that of usefulness or utility. A friend will be selected because of what he or she can provide—for example, access to a particular club or group, or a car to get back and forth.

I can appreciate the fact that many of us might, on first glance, be appalled by such a practice. "I can't believe that it is O.K. for my child to use somebody else just to get a car ride!"

While I am not trying to condone such a pragmatic or utilitarian view of friendship, I do want to point out the simple fact that quite often the reason some of us join forces is because of the usefulness of such a relationship. If you and I can appreciate that such utility is often the initial drawing card, while at the same time understanding that relationships need to be mutual, with give and take on *both* sides, then perhaps we will be positioned to assist our teens in initiating the contact they desire.

I can remember Tina, who at the age of sixteen was the first in her class to get her license. Being able to drive to school and go to the mall served as a major factor in Tina's immediate increase in popularity. It is possible that many teens will misunderstand the base upon which they have become popular and thus make themselves very vulnerable to being used and being rejected as others gain access to a license. For Tina, however, such was not the case. She was quite aware that her increased worth was a matter of her access to a car. However, she was also quite clear that this access provided her an avenue to meet people and spend time with individuals that previously she had little in common with. Further, Tina was able to use her temporary power to begin relationships. Many of these relationships ceased because they were only founded on Tina's providing transportation (no give and take). Others, which may have started out on this level, matured to the point where she enjoyed the company and the activities of the others, and they enjoyed being with her (not simply being driven by her).

When my children were small I know I would help them to share, to let others use their things. Sharing is a very Christian act. Sharing is also a way of developing relationships. When I can provide you with something you like or need, be it advice or my album, *and* you can provide me with something in return, be it your availability or your record, we begin to see the value of interacting. From these very superficial levels of relating and sharing of tangibles, we may slowly develop and progress to deeper relating and sharing of self.

Again as an informed parent, I may be able to help my child share the tangibles as an initial step to meeting and making friends. With this knowledge I may be more receptive to opening up my home for the "rap session" or the "record listening" or the after-school get-together. Similarly, I may allow my teen to use the car to go to the mall, or may volunteer to be the parent of the teen who is willing to drive!

If we can communicate with our teens and begin to identify what they and their peers value or need, then together, as in the previous situation with Tom, we can develop strategies for increasing their surface value and assist them in gaining entrance into the desired group of friends. The development and maintenance of real friendships will take more than such simple, superficial sharing, but it is a start.

Similarity. Often a friend is one with whom our youth shares many similar interests. While opposites may attract, the relationships that endure are those where we share something in common. Sports, music, movies, work and many other interests often provide the basis upon which a peer relationship is established.

Once the group has been established there is generally a strong push to highlight such similarity through the shared use of slang, certain behavior mannerisms, and wearing club jackets, rock-group pins, etc. Further there is often a strong force within the group to have all of the members continue to share similarly through conforming to group rules of behavior. Such conformity has been the basis for the bad press that peer groups often receive.

It is often true that our teens will engage in some negative conformity. Cursing, smoking, and drinking are just a few of the activities and behaviors which can result from negative conformity. But just as a peer group can influence our teen to engage in negative behaviors, so it can also be a strong force for positive behaviors. A group which values taking care of their bodies through eating well and exercise, or a group which is motivated to achieve in sports or academics, will reinforce these attitudes and behaviors in all of its members.

Because of the attraction to the similar, we need to be more aware of our teens' positive, growthful interest. We also need to assist them in developing these interests and maintaining the relationships which form as a result of these interests. This will be the best defense against the development of relationships and interests which are potentially unhealthy and destructive.

Carting our teen to sports practices and games, dance classes, karate lessons, computer clubs or band practices can be an exhausting experience for parents. The payoff of seeing our teens succeed at positive activities and engage with others around such healthy activities will more than compensate for our efforts.

I know that my wife is more than tired of carting drums and bass guitar from house to house, or from home to school. Similarly, there are times when I'm not sure I could take one more hour of band practice. However, the interest my sons Kristian and Drew have developed for music has introduced them to a number of really special friends. When I see their excitement over playing in the "battle of the bands," the camaraderie between John and Kristian, their inclusion of the "little brother–bass player" into plans to attend concerts, or work on songs, etc., it is clear that the loud practice sessions and the miles driven are small payment for such healthy peer interaction.

Compensation. While most often our teens identify and join forces with those who share similarity, there are times when a peer or a peer group is used as a compensation for something which our teens feel they are lacking.

Eric is fourteen years old. He is bright, yet underachieving. He is tall and quite thin. Eric is clumsy both physically and socially. He feels out of step with the rest of his peers and assumes that they all think he is weird. Recently the school has reported that Eric is "hanging out" with a bad group of kids. He has started to act up in class, making noises and acting quite disrespectful to his teachers when they correct him. Eric's parents told me that he was changing. He no longer wants to be around his parents, and often speaks quite disrespectfully to them.

When I met Eric he seemed open and friendly in discussion. Quite early in our discussions it became apparent that Eric felt that the group he was now hanging out with gave him power. He stated quite clearly, "Nobody laughs at me anymore; they know I'm bad, so they leave me alone."

For Eric the group compensated for his own sense of weakness and his perceived impotence. Eric felt that he was unable to gain the respect of his teachers, his peers, and even his parents. But even though he was unable to gain the respect of others as an individual, he felt that being a part of this group provided the power, the strength that he needed.

Teens who feel inadequate or inferior and who sense that they are unable to gain acceptance or respect or prove successful in their efforts are vulnerable to the influence of a peer group. Some, like Eric, will do and say anything the group requires since they see the group as essential to their sense of support and power. Other teens may find a group of peers who are somewhat less powerful than they are. By identifying with less bright, or less talented, or even younger peers, the youth who was previously feeling inferior can now emerge as a leader. Being looked up to, even if it is by children much younger or more immature than oneself, is seen as better than being looked down upon by one's peers.

Associating with peers for their compensatory value is not always so negative. Quite often teens recognize that a particular group of peers possess the attitude or skills they lack and thus they see the group as providing the learning models and the opportunities for successfully satisfying normal, healthy desires. Take Linda, for example. Linda is fifteen years old. In my estimation she is quite attractive, somewhat thin and a very pleasant teen. Linda, however, sees herself as somewhat unattractive, with no shape whatsoever. Although Linda would like to meet and eventually date boys, her own poor body image and anxiety about interacting with boys prevents her from initiating social contact.

Recently Linda has become associated with a group of girls who are collectively viewed as quite popular and active in school. Through this association Linda has come in contact with a number of boys. While standing with her friends at lunch, Linda has been able to watch them interact, model that interaction and has recently begun to feel much more secure and willing to initiate contact with boys. For Linda, the group provided the opportunity and safety needed for learning social, interpersonal skills. This particular group compensated for Linda's limited social skills and lack of personal initiative.

Knowing that our teens may be associating with a particular group out of a need to compensate for their real or perceived weakness provides us with some direction for further supporting them. We need to help our teens identify the need being met by the group. If we can identify that the value of the group rests in our teens' faulty perception of their own limitations, we need to help them reassess their own capabilities in light of the evidence we can provide. If, however, our teens have accurately identified a real area of weakness or limitation, we need to assist them in identifying a number of ways to compensate for that weakness (including using the peer group), and assist them to identify the pros and cons for each method of compensation. Thus the teens who find that the group helps them "come on to" and feel comfortable interacting with the opposite sex may also recognize that the group requires them to stay away from some of their other "older" friends, or that the former group has given them a bad reputation. Under these circumstances we may be able to discuss other strategies for compensating for our teens' insecurities, including finding another peer group which won't have the negatives attached and which can still provide the support they seek.

But Why That Group?

For many parents the issue isn't whether their teens should have a peer group, or even be influenced by their peers. For many of us the issue is: "Why that group?"

We seem to ask ourselves: "If this is such an important time to be establishing meaningful relationships, why must my teens pick such undesirables?" Whenever I hear or even speak such a question, I am quick to remind myself that our teens' undesirable friend is the child of other parents. I wonder if those parents have the same question regarding the desirability of my own child for their youth. But even with such considerations we must accept the fact that some peers may prove detrimental to our own child's healthy growth and development. Under these circumstances we are most likely to ask "Why this group?" and *"What's a parent to do?"*

When our teen begins to identify with another who in our estimation is not the type of child we want our teen to be associated with, we need to step back and attempt to clarify the issues to which we are reacting. Once we have concretely identified our concern, we need to share that concern with our teen—not as a dictate or a command that he or she no longer associate with this youth, but rather as a point of concern to be discussed. It is essential that we come to identify which of our teen's "needs" are being satisfied by this particular association, so that we may begin to find alternative ways to satisfy that need. For example, if our teen states that he and his friend are very much alike, then perhaps it is our judgment which needs correcting. Under these circumstances it is important that we begin to have contact with this youth in order to experience the similarities and discover what it is which our teen values in this other.

We may find however that our youth's association is based on what the other can provide him or her. Under these conditions we will find it much more useful in guiding our teen by providing an alternative, more acceptable means of satisfying these needs than we will by prohibiting future contact with the friend. Quite often a youth who is attempting to make a statement about his or her own independence will react even more strongly to a group of unacceptable peers when Mom and Dad seem to have a strong negative reaction to that association.

The above should not be interpreted as implying that we should not screen or be concerned about who it is that our teen seeks out as friends. On the contrary, given the potential for influence among peers, it is essential that we know the peers with whom our teen associates. What is being suggested, however, is that simply prohibiting contact or association with one or another youth will most often prove unsuccessful, and could prove counter-productive. Our attempts at restricting contact may make those peers all that much more desirable.

While being concerned about the potentially negative influence some peers may have on our youth, we must be cautious to avoid prejudgment. As such I encourage parents who express a concern over the possible negative influence that a particular youth or peer group may have on their teen to sit with their adolescent and calmly and objectively draft a listing of "symptoms" which could be used to define the effects of negative influence. Quite often such a list would include things such as lower grades in school, getting in trouble with the police, breaking home rules such as time curfews, developing unacceptable habits such as smoking, etc. It is important that this list include factors considered important by parents and the teen.

When such a list can be developed and the parents agree to let the teens use their own judgment to pick their friends, as long as there are no signs or symptoms of negative influence, then not only have the parents affirmed the teens' right to be self-directed but they have assisted them in developing a rational process for assessing the potential for future problems. Further when the list is created collaboratively by parents and teens during the early stage of the relationship then it can be used as an objective tool for knowing if and when to terminate contact.

Parent Points

- With an emerging sense of "who they are," our teens seek to share this "self" with others by belonging.
- Peer groups are the essential beginnings of tomorrow's families, tomorrow's society.
- Peer groups serve as:
  **an arena to learn new skills,
  **an opportunity to practice skills of sharing, belonging and intimacy,
  **a mechanism for receiving feedback about who I am and how I am perceived.
- Peer groups serve as a place for need satisfaction.
- Peer groups can compensate for teen limitations and shortcomings.
- Peers exert extreme pressure to conform.
- Conformity to peer pressure can take on both negative and positive qualities:
  **Teens who feel insecure or inadequate are more vulnerable to negative peer pressure.
  **Teens who are unable to identify alternative ways to meet their needs may be more vulnerable to negative peer pressure.
- Identify the value for our teens' peers and assist them to identify the costs and rewards for peer involvement.

- **In addition to assisting our teens to recognize the costs and rewards for particular peer involvement, we need to assist them in identifying alternative means for need satisfaction.**

- **Friends are chosen because of their similarity, their utility or their ability to compensate for my own limitations.**

- **Assist our teens in choosing relationships which are healthy, and avoid those of negative influence. Prohibition alone will often prove counter-productive. Rather than prohibition, we need to:**
  ****be able to communicate our concerns to our teens,**
  ****invite our teens to identify the needs being met through this association,**
  ****work with our teens collaboratively to find additional strategies for need satisfaction.**

9.

When Crisis Occurs

What did we do? My God, where did we go wrong?

The early years of parenting were filled with many minor "crises." Like most of you, my wife Karen and I have sat in emergency rooms as we watched open wounds being stitched and broken bones cast. We have all known nights of fatigue and bewilderment as we bellowed our parental directive "to go to bed and stay there!" Crises are certainly part of the parenting experience.

Our children have also experienced their share of "crises." Throughout their development they have known moments of fear and anxiety associated with going to school for the first time, sensing a "monster" in their room, or simply having to wait for the results of their test grade. They have experienced intense anger and frustration when not allowed to stay up or to go to the mall, or when simply told "No!"

For both parents and children such crises are part and parcel of the living experience. We struggle and yet we grow through such normative or normal crises.

Often, however, our struggle leads us not to growth but to the brink of self-destruction. A teen's addictive involvement with drugs and alcohol or an experience of disappointment which turns to despair and suicidal ideation is no longer a normal or growthful crisis. The frustration of a no which escalates to hostile words and actions between father and son and ends in physical attack and abuse are signs not of growth but of destruction.

When such a destructive crisis occurs, many parents turn inward in doubt, guilt and fear. They become absorbed in questions of "Why us?" or "Where did we go wrong?" Rather than questions of self-doubt and blame, we need to consider the question, "What is a parent to do?" The current chapter looks at the issues of when and where to turn for help.

Knowing When Help Is Needed

The answer to the question: "When should we seek professional help for our teens?" is simply, *"When they ask for it!"* Most parents are surprised to find that many teens who have been troubled by an issue in their life and are experiencing difficulty coping are quite willing to seek out professional help. Not all teens, however, who need assistance will ask for it *directly.* Often their request comes in symbolic and symptomatic form.

Gwen (age fifteen) is just such an example of indirectly requesting help. Gwen started slowly, noting that she needed to lose a few pounds for summer. She would ask for small amounts of food at dinner, but soon started missing dinner altogether. When asked what she wanted for breakfast or lunch, she would note that she would grab something at school. Gwen's original concern for dropping five or ten pounds from her already slim 115 pound stature soon became an obsession to lose thirty pounds. With the increased weight loss goal, Gwen began to use extreme weight loss techniques. She exercised excessively, often doing aerobics for two hours a day, and actively refused to eat.

Clearly what might have started as a normative adolescent crisis over body image and weight became an anorexic nightmare. For Gwen, her parents' concerns and efforts to assist her were not enough. Even though she protested that everything was fine and that she didn't need any help, professional assistance was clearly necessary.

Our teens' cries for help come in a variety of forms. Knowing some of the more typical signs of trouble can help us to respond to their request for help. These signs may include an increase in physical complaints such as headaches, stomachaches or muscle pains which upon inspection fail to have any organic cause. Our teens may begin to withdraw from social contact with family and friends. They may appear extremely lethargic, fatigued or despondent. Radical changes in patterns of eating, sleeping or engaging in recreation may also signal the existence of some troublesome concern for our youth. The list is not intended to be exhaustive, but it is at least representative of the type of changes in our teens' behavior which may prove symptomatic of some deeper, more disturbing concern. The longer the list of symptoms, the less mature or age-appropriate our teens' actions, and the longer the duration of this condition, the more important it is to seek assistance.

We must remember that wide mood swings and somewhat radical shifts in our teens' behavior are typical and to be expected. However a general test of normality is when the behavior chosen appears to be similar to that exhibited by most others in that age group and when it promotes ongoing maturation and successful adaptation to the stress of adolescence. If, however, our teens' behavior is very different from their peers and it is causing them to have increased difficulty coping with the typical demands of peers, family and school, then professional assistance may be required.

Often it is not our teens but we, the parents, who need professional assistance. Parenting an adolescent can be a very stressful experience. Our own insecurities, apprehensions and concerns about parenting an adolescent may serve as a major clue that professional assistance is needed. Sometimes one or two interviews with a professional can make a world of difference to the anxious and concerned parent.

Further, our feelings of uneasiness may prove to be a sensitive diagnostic tool. In our discussion with a professional we may find that our concerns are very well founded. We may come to realize that our own reactions are in response to some very early warning signals being sent by our teens. The earlier we can detect such signs, the more chance we have of preventing the onset of more serious symptoms. Thus I would have to agree with the adage that an "ounce of prevention is worth a pound of cure."

Even when our teens do not exhibit signs of "trouble" we should feel free to seek professional consultation whenever we feel that such consultation may ease our own parenting anxieties.

Where To Turn

Once we have accepted the fact that professional assistance is desired, we may be flooded by a series of questions: "Whom do we contact?" "How much will it cost?" "How long will it take?" "What's the difference between this professional and that?" "How do we begin?"

Unless you have had personal experience with counseling or psychotherapy, the above questions may appear quite overwhelming. One place to turn initially might be your own local school district. The public school system will most likely have a counseling office or pupil personnel service department. These individuals may be called by different titles such as Guidance Counselor, School Psychologist, Social Worker or Special Education Preventionist. While they may be unable to provide direct, extensive service for you and your teen, they will often be quite familiar with the various mental health services available in your community. The state or city Department of Health or Department of Mental Health is also another primary source of referral information. These agencies are most often listed in the phone directory and are available without cost or with fees established on the ability to pay.

Should you seek private, individual professional assistance you may want to look for an individual who not only has training in the area of human development and mental health, but who also has had special training or experience in the area of adolescence. Again, there are a variety of professionals who are trained to provide such assistance. A psychiatrist is a physician who has had additional training, beyond his or her general medical training, in the area of psychology. As physicians they can prescribe medication where such may be indicated. A psychologist is an individual with a master's degree or most often a doctorate (Ph.D., Ed.D. or Psy.D. degree). While referred to as "doctor" these individuals cannot prescribe medication but will work along with a medical doctor if such medication is required. Mental health counselors, social workers and pastoral counselors are additional professionals who may have special training in the area of counseling adolescents and their family. The title of such individuals is less important than is their educational backgound, their training, and their experience in working with teens. Once a counselor/therapist with the proper qualification has been identified, then the most important criteria would be the degree to which you and your teen are able to develop a sense of confidence and rapport with the individual.

Seeking Help and Feeling O.K. About It

Parenting, as was noted early in the book, is not an innate skill. Successfully addressing all of the problems presented in the course of our parenting requires the development of knowledge and much skill. However, sometimes our skills and our understanding of adolescent development is simply not enough. Sometimes we need the assistance of a professional in order to assist us and our teens over a particular hurdle to their development.

If we keep our perspective and our values clear, we will remember that it is our children's health and well-being which is primary and not our own desire to appear totally adequate and competent as parents. Most parents today feel less of a sense of personal failure about seeking professional assistance than in the past. Most of us recognize that we are simply not prepared to help our teens through all of the crises and problems they may experience in their development. Further, most of us accept that such a limitation to our parenting skill is nothing which we need to feel ashamed of or embarrassed about.

Just as we do not hesitate to seek medical assistance when our teens are ill, we need to feel free to seek emotional and psychological assistance when they are troubled. When we can get over our sense of guilt and defeat when something goes wrong in their normal development, we will be better able to take the steps needed to return them and ourselves back to healthy development. Seeking a professional who is trained and experienced with adolescents may be that essential step.

Parent Points

- Crises in childhood are to be expected; growth and maturation are often the outcome of "normative" crises.

- Sometimes crises are overwhelming to our youth. They stagnate in response and appear fixed and unable to cope. Under these conditions, they and we need professional assistance.

- We *should* seek professional help and assistance when:
  **Our teen directly asks for help.
  **Our teen indirectly asks for help by exhibiting symptoms of distress, such as:
    (1) somatic complaints (e.g., headaches, muscle pains or stomachaches),
    (2) withdrawal from normal contact with family and friends,
    (3) loss of energy and showing an apparent depressed mood,
    (4) *sudden* loss of interest in previously engaged activities or pastimes,
    (5) radical change in eating or sleeping patterns.
  **Anytime we, as parents, sense a need for guidance and support.

- Seeking professional assistance *does not* mean:
  **we or our children are crazy,
  **we failed as parents or they failed as teens,
  **we or they will be labeled and stigmatized for the remainder of our days.

- **We may find guidance and assistance by contacting:**
  ****school personnel such as the principal, guidance counselors, school psychologist, chaplain, social worker or prevention specialist.**
  ****state and local mental health departments which will be listed in the phone book.**
  ****private mental health practitioners such as a licensed psychologist, psychiatrist, clinical social worker, pastoral counselor, etc.**

- **When seeking assistance we should seek professionals who have the education, clinical training, and experience working with adolescents and with whom we and our teen feel confident and have rapport.**

- **Seeking help for a problem is a sign of mature, rational problem solving as well as a sign of love and concern.**

Epilogue: Learning, Living, Loving

She's so grown, so beautiful. She is really quite a woman, no longer a child! Where did our baby go?
(Mother of an eighteen year old)

Yes, where did our babies go? For me it only seems like yesterday that I was sharing the news with my wife that we were about to become parents. During the fifteen years following the birth of my son Kristian, I have experienced much *learning,* much *living,* but most importantly much *loving.*

Too many of my memories, and perhaps too much of this book, overlook the learning, the living and the loving which has passed. Too often we lock into the "problems" of raising a teen, to the exclusion of the joy and mystery of parenting.

The clumsiness of the emerging athlete or the dropping grades of our "socialite" have occupied too much of our attention. Our concerns over their clothes or length of hair have blinded us to the beauty and magic of the emerging adult.

For many of us, looking at our teen is an experience of finding fault or potential disaster. We need to expand our view of adolescence so that it is no longer narrowly defined in terms of pain, destruction and disappointment. Surely the road traveled by our teen is filled with problems and potential disasters, but it is also blessed with new joys, new potential and growth.

While this book is coming to an end, the learning, the living, and the loving will continue.

For our teen, the search continues. As our child emerges from the teen years, options of desired hair style, vocational choices, and circle of friends have most likely been narrowed.

Our teen enters adulthood with a sense of identity and direction. The search for self is far from complete, however.

The process of identification of oneself continues throughout a lifetime. Our youth, therefore, will still need to challenge rules and values, try on new behaviors and styles. They may reject many of the old, proven ways of our family's tradition. Such continued "trying on" is necessary for our teens to eventually identify that which is truly theirs.

As the vision of self becomes clearer, so does the desire to share this self with another, in true intimacy. Our teen will travel beyond puppy-love and crushes to developing deeply personal and meaningful relationships. Relationships founded on genuineness and openness will endure, whereas those less mature relationships founded on utility, compensation or surface similarity will fade.

As with others in our teen's sphere of contact, we will also be invited to relate. The "person" of our son and daughter will wish to establish a meaningful, genuine relationship with us as people, not simply as parents. For this to occur we will need to step outside of our role and from beneath our mask as parent, and allow our son or daughter to know the me beneath.

Such unveiling can be a very scary and risky event. For just as Dorothy's unveiling of the man behind the Wizard in Oz revealed his imperfections, so too will our own less desirable human traits become obvious. Stepping from behind the role of parent opens us up to be discovered as truly human, with all our fears, our inadequacies and our frailties. But stepping from behind this barrier also allows us to come to truly know and share with this other, our child. Just as we will be demasked by our youth and can emerge with a truly personal, loving relationship with him or her, so too will our God.

Our teens will attempt to unmask the God of our formal church, or our family tradition. They may actively resist attending services, or try to discount the value of the Scriptures and prayer. However, as they travel their road toward identity, they will have the opportunity to understand that each painful and joyful encounter has been an event in which the Lord spoke to them in a special way.

The road will continue. It will challenge our youth to clarify who they are and who they are to become. Further, their road will lead them into relationships which are deeply personal and intimate. It is in this sharing of self that our teens will come to develop a special, personal relationship with their God.

What's a Parent To Do?

Just as our children's journey is not complete, neither is ours. As parents we will need to encourage our teens to take time out of their frantic search, time to reflect, time to renew and time to respond to the new challenges. Our teens need to step back from their eager search for careers, for friends, for the answers to their many questions, so as to quiet the search and become faithful listeners. Christ is calling them to a personal relationship, but they need to hear!

We need to invite them to rest and reflect on what they have learned, how they have lived and how they can love. We need to assist them in letting go of their daily concerns and making themselves available to relationship with the Lord.

Our teens will need help in learning how to quiet themselves and make themselves open to their unique "life call." Finding the Lord in themselves and in their relationship with others and positioning themselves for a personal response to this invitation to "come, follow me" is the task our teens will soon confront.

As Christian parents our task is to teach our teens to pray, to contemplate Jesus and to prepare to respond to the special invitation which Jesus offers.

Our task is to help them see the very special ways Christ has called them to learn, to live, and to *love!*